The Way
of
Adventure

The Way
of
Adventure

*Transforming Your Life and Work
with Spirit and Vision*

JEFF SALZ, PH.D.

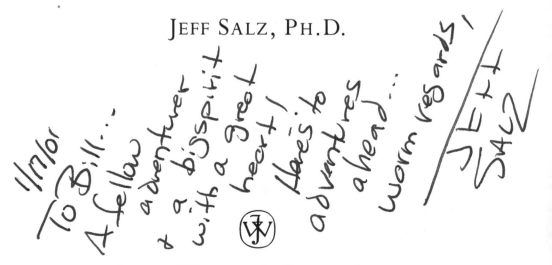

1/17/01
To Bill...
A fellow
adventurer
& a big spirit
with a great
heart!
Here's to
adventures
ahead...
warm regards
Jeff Salz

JOHN WILEY & SONS, INC.
New York • Chichester • Weinheim • Brisbane • Singapore • Toronto

Published by John Wiley & Sons, Inc.
Published simultaneously in Canada

Design and production by Navta Associates, Inc.

Grateful acknowledgment is made for the following: "Freakin' at the Freaker's Ball," words and music by Shel Silverstein, copyright © 1972 (renewed) by Evil Eye Music, Inc., Daytona Beach, Fla., used by permission; photograph of the boat on Lake Titicaca by permission of the photographer Nevada Wier; four lines from "Leap Before You Look," from *W. H. Auden Collected Poems* by W. H. Auden, copyright © 1945 by W. H. Auden, reprinted by permission of Random House Inc. and Faber and Faber Ltd.

This publication is designed to provide accurate and authoritative information in regard to the subject matter covered. It is sold with the understanding that the publisher is not engaged in rendering professional services. If professional advice or other expert assistance is required, the services of a competent professional person should be sought.

Library of Congress Cataloging-in-Publication Data

Salz, Jeff.
    The way of adventure : transforming your life and work with spirit and vision / Jeff Salz.
      p. cm.
    ISBN 0-471-38758-4 (cloth : alk. paper)
     1. Self-realization.   2. Conduct of life.   3. Adventure and adventurers— Miscellanea.   I. Title.

BJ1470 .S323   2000
158—dc21   00-039232

For Kate, who held the vision

CONTENTS

THE SECOND STEP

Aim Higher Than Everest

THE SIXTH STEP

Enjoy the View

ACKNOWLEDGMENTS

If I know anything to be true in the realm of human endeavor, it is that the popular image of the heroic solo adventurer is an illusion. We do nothing of any consequence alone. In writing this book, as in every mountain I have ever climbed, I have been supported, accompanied, and inspired every step of the way by a host of teammates too numerous to name completely.

Immediately and foremost, I've got to toast my dear friends—who also happen to be my agent and editor, respectively—Laurie Fox and D. Patrick Miller. It is only through your belief, artistry, and hard work that I have gotten to the stage where I get to write any acknowledgments at all.

To all those amazing people whose stories appear in this book, I thank you deeply for giving freely of your time. In addition, I need to thank a few other members of the expedition for specific gifts of inspiration.

Stephen Meyers, my perpetual adventure buddy from Mongolia to Bolivia, for countless moments of camaraderie—but especially the day, as we rode our horses through the Amazon jungle in search of tapirs and toucans, you convinced me to keep on writing. Karen Christiansen, wherever you are, for keeping literary sparks aglow while some very wet weather beat down on my lonely Covelo trailer. My old professor of folk study, the infinitely compassionate Ben Levine, for first sending me to South America, tape recorder in hand. Joe Robinson, fellow travel junkie and editor/publisher of *Escape*, for faithfully nurturing my literary urges for nearly a decade. My big brother Ken Dychtwald, for handing me a candle in a particularly dark night of the soul, and now, years later, regularly checking in to make sure it's still lit. John Azzaro—part gaucho and part Groucho—for fueling my success as a professional speaker with his relentless spirit of service and love of laughter. Personal mentors Layne Longfellow and Paul Brenner, two of the truly great men I know, for modeling the truth that while adventure may be the path, character is the destination.

My family is the home team that has helped me make dreams come true. My incredible mom and dad, Lenore and Edward Salz, inspired my desire to understand and experience the world and even paid for my plane ticket to New Zealand after I left home at sixteen. Thanks to the ever supportive Dlugasch clan—Carole, David, Howard—but especially Jana, for helping out in Cadaqués, Spain, when, possessed by the muse, I spent a month in my pajamas attached to a laptop by my fingertips. And to my offspring Yeshe and Jacinto for watching countless Barney videos with the volume turned down to barely audible levels. They will now get their daddy back—and a lot fewer Barney videos. Of course, my sweet lady, life mate, and pal Kate Pruefer, for being both an incredible "proofer" and the best partner a boy could have.

To all my dear friends for all the companionship and encouragement along the trail. Thanks for saving my posterior in countless ways on innumerable occasions over the years. You know who you are and that I am not exaggerating. Considering all we've been through, it's a miracle any of us are still here at all. Lydia and Chato Ulloa, though you are no longer with us, thanks for becoming my Mexican mom and dad, giving me a place to do nothing but write for months at a time and helping me bridge worlds with not just my head but my heart. Your generous and loving spirits live on in these pages. The next book will be about you.

Thanks to Mark Chimsky at Editorial Plus and the fine folks at the Linda Chester Agency for fanning flickering embers into flame. Finally, here's to Tom Miller, my editor at Wiley, whose applied alchemy of faith and vision converted a conflagration into a controlled burn, for bringing this book safely into the world. Without him, I'd still be in *midwife* crisis.

Hey, I almost forgot . . . thank *you*. Not just for picking up this book but for a willingness to look at life as a great adventure. You see, if enough of us buy not just the book but the concept, we may yet be able to jump on, grab the reins, and wheel this whole wild world around into some entirely new direction. After all, that's the ultimate adventure.

The Way
of
Adventure

Why Adventure?

They may call it by different names and search for it in different locales, but all adventurers hope to find their Shangri-La—the exotic destination that fulfills all their yearning. Yet the most exotic destination of all is the one to be found within your own adventurous spirit —after you've put yourself to the test and found hidden reserves of creativity, resourcefulness, and perseverance.

This book is about facing everyday life, work, and relationships with the spirit of adventure. And one thing is certain: most folks in modern civilization are seriously in need of adventure. Never before has a species been locked in a struggle with its own datebooks for survival. We are moving so fast that the phrase human race has taken on a new meaning; each day we feel as though we are falling farther and farther behind. And there is a modem to our madness. Plugged into phones, television, and computer screens during waking hours, we grow simultaneously information-rich and experience-poor. The joy of living seems to be passing us by while we depend on action movies, amusement park rides, and close calls on the freeway to provide us with occasional thrills.

A spirit of adventure is the joyful determination to go out and rediscover life for ourselves, finding peak experiences in situations and environments that may have previously seemed mundane. The traditional adventure has a basic template: modern people traveling by ancient methods over great distances to places that they have no practical reason to go. To this indulgence, I plead guilty. And it's great fun to do—but it's been done. Adventurers who have sallied forth with no other purpose than reaching their exotic destination usually report disappointment when they reach the goal. If your physical adventure is not following the internal map of a spiritual adventure, you might as well not go anywhere.

I've spent most of my life wandering the planet, mostly on foot, asking people, "What is the meaning of life?" For some thirty years now, tape recorder in hand, I've sought out the most spirited incarnations of humanity in the wildest corners of the earth. I've interviewed nomads on the steppes of Outer Mongolia, Chilean fishermen in their boats off Tierra del Fuego, Mayan Indians in the hills of Chiapas, and Buddhist monks in the hidden monasteries of Nepal. You'll meet some of these people later in the book.

Then I realized that I had been selling my own people short. So I began asking the same questions of shining stars closer to home: individuals from many walks of modern life who are making their mark in brave and adventurous ways. I interviewed explorers, businesspeople, inventors, artists, athletes, political consultants, and even a three-star general. Then came the fun of making connections: what did the skill set of a Peruvian healer—whose tools are swords, staffs, and guinea pigs—have in common with the American inventor whose company produces defense systems? What did the musings of a Bolivian peasant on the shores of Lake Titicaca have in common with the philosophy of the meditation guru for the Chicago Bulls? What beliefs and practices were shared by a Tibetan lama and an international political consultant?

As I began organizing these comparisons in this book, I realized that I was putting together what Philip Staniford would have described as an adventure in transpersonal anthropology. Before I define my terms, let me describe the man.

The late Philip Staniford was my friend and mentor. We taught classes together at San Diego State University. A doctor of anthropology, he described himself as a "journeyman chronicler, bard, artist, and pilgrim." Editor of *Phoenix: Journal of Transpersonal Anthropology*, he was a wonderfully unusual scientist, a true pioneer who enjoyed the questions more than the answers. His trademarks were a belly laugh and a curious expression that cast doubt on every serious assumption, plus a fistful of rainbow pens that brought color to everything he touched.

Philip was an explorer in the truest sense of the word, continually venturing beyond the easy outposts of human knowledge. "Human consciousness in general and anthropologists in particular are at an exciting crossroads," he said. "The most meaningful contributions anthropologists can make to current affairs is to show viable alternatives to the Greco-Judeo-Christian and scientific cultural realities we take for granted. We know and can demonstrate the richness and appropriateness of Hopi, Cheyenne, Eskimo, Japanese, Tibetan, and many other ways. By experiencing their modes of imaging and being for ourselves, we may stretch our ordinary horizons and strategies to include aspects of being beyond ordinary Western ways."

This book is a voyage to discover some of the "metavalues"—truths extending beyond time and place—that lend our lives both substance and song, not just success but satisfaction. Transpersonal anthropology—loosely defined as the study of the qualities, properties, and possibilities of human nature that underlie but extend beyond all restrictive boundaries of culture, transcending any specific and prescribed set of values or beliefs—is our craft.

Adventure Is an Inside Job

What constitutes an adventure in my book is any intentional experience that substantially alters our perspective long enough to see things we have never before seen—and to see familiar things in ways we have never before seen them. In times of great transitions such as ours this kind of view is essential for our continued viability as a species.

In a Faustian bargain with life's prosaic demands we all too often find ourselves trading our child's innocence and receptivity for hardened stoicism. Adventure is the antidote. It is a bucket of cold water thrown over our comfortably slumbering souls. Without deliberate leaps of faith and dances of derring-do, we may survive . . . but that is all.

Unlike the Arctic explorer whose objective is simply to travel over vast distances, moving his body like a marker across the empty landscape, the efficient adventurer of the spirit learns to cover the most inner ground in the least physical distance. Traveling around the world, we will awaken someday and poke our heads from the tent in a yak pasture at 12,000 feet only to discover that we have arrived in someone else's backyard—or living room. And that's when it dawns on us that real adventure is an inside job.

It is an ironic but timeless truth that we often require a pilgrimage to Patagonia, Pakistan, or Papua New Guinea in order to discover the treasure that has long awaited us in our own home, hidden behind our own hearth. Adventure is either in our hearts and minds, or it is nowhere at all.

Because I've been something of a daredevil wanderer with a postgraduate degree, it's not unusual to hear myself compared to another professor-explorer, Indiana Jones. But I like to remind people that I am far closer in style and character to another Steven Spielberg invention, the knobby-faced, wide-eyed alien called ET. While Indy wields a bullwhip and pistol, ET makes friends and influences terrestrials with his innocence, ineptness, and obvious need for assistance.

I know by firsthand experience that upon arrival in a new world—where one can face everything from the suspicion of the locals to the acquisitiveness of well-armed bandits—a show of force is far less effective (and a lot more dangerous) than a display of genuine guilelessness. There is nothing like falling off your horse or tripping over your own feet to swing loyalties and sympathies your way.

I offer in this book some expeditionary advice for successfully navigating through the single certainty in life: uncertainty. Surely nothing has changed in recent times like change itself. While in the old days it was only the world explorer who had to deal with untraveled environments and unforeseeable outcomes, now it is essential for everyone to have this skill set. Drawn from a few decades of extreme exploits over earth, water and ice from west of Ushuaia to east of Ulan Bator, I hope to lend you some techniques for mastering ever shifting circumstances. The fact that I have lived long enough to tender such advice is a testimonial to the fact that they work.

The way of adventure invites us to define ourselves through action, not just words. Adventurers tend to have short attention spans. They insist on the steepest, most direct path up the mountain. You get there faster, they are likely to explain, and the process itself invigorates. The way of adventure encourages us to experiment, to press onward and upward to discover how the view just keeps getting better. It is useful for those who know that the edge is where the view is best, where all growth and learning take place.

As a mountaineer prone to solo jaunts, I have come upon glorious clusters of flowers in a hanging valley so remote that I am certain no one else will ever glimpse them. Alone, having known these flowers, I have realized a certain responsibility to carry their beauty along in spirit to share with others. Similarly, I have met a few people in the wildest recesses—among the poorest, most disenfranchised of our species—whose fire and kindness deserve to be honored. My undying belief that there is hope for this wayward planet stems from the courage, dignity, caring, and innocence I have experienced in their presence.

I have spent many a night with humble folks who could not answer my questions about the "meaning of life" but lived it, danced it, celebrated it before my eyes. More than once I found myself hiding money under a dinner plate—the equivalent of a week's wages for the locals—in an attempt to repay their kindness. Almost as often I was later chased down a trail by my host or hostess, pesos in hand, scolding, "Gringo! This meal was not for sale!" The meal was for love.

This book is dedicated to the vanishing wild people and places of the earth. It is a plea that the meek, if not allowed to inherit the earth, should at least be able to abide here peacefully. Our turbocharged society seems bent on destroying the very seeds of our salvation: the boundless natural wisdom and diversity of wilderness and native peoples. If I were to dedicate every waking hour to the task of returning in kind all the beauty and generosity I have been offered, it would still never be enough. This book is a small down payment for an immense debt of gratitude.

At 3 A.M. over tacos in a very bad part of Mexico City, someone once told me, "La nobleza no conoce fronteras": The human heart knows no bounds. To experience the kindness of a stranger in a strange land is really not that uncommon, yet for me it has become the reason I travel. I don't know if I had stayed at home if I ever would have learned the secret whispered to me that night on the lamplit streets of Mexico. *La nobleza no conoce fronteras.*

Somewhere along the trail we discover that, like the faintest of stars in a bright firmament, happiness is best seen out of the corner of our eye. Pursued directly as a primary goal, happiness becomes only a source of frustration. Yet it is likely to blossom fully in our lives as a by-product of a life of service. After some exploration we learn that our greatest joy comes not from self-seeking but in "other-serving."

I first learned this lesson by transcribing many hours of taped conversations with Mapuche Indians, Chilean *huasos*, and wealthy Argentine *estancieros* during a year of foot travel through South America. Having queried all these people about the meaning of life, I finally found the common denominator in their replies: *trabajo.* Work. Not work defined as "that thing we do to earn the money to get the material possessions we want that will ultimately make us happy," but work as defined by Kahlil Gibran, the Lebanese poet and mystic, who said that work is "love made visible."

The question for the modern adventurer of the spirit is how to change everyday work from the first kind to the second kind. How do we redesign both our attitudes and our work environments so that our daily work is experienced as a precious opportunity to make a difference in the lives of those around us? Whether we work at home, in an office, or in the wide open spaces, can work itself become our higher-than-Everest challenge?

The Buddha taught that beyond fulfilling our own basic needs, there are two other reasons for working. First, through our efforts we bring goods and services into the world that contribute to the well-being and spiritual evolution of others. Second, the necessity of having to earn a living requires us to work in concert with our fellows, helping us to overcome our innate tendencies toward self-centeredness and isolation. Most of us spend the majority of our waking hours working. That's why I hope you'll be able to apply the lessons of this book to your own work experience, transforming work from a mundane duty or drudge to an ongoing exploit that calls upon your creativity, resourcefulness, and perseverance.

How to Use This Book

This book has been organized so that you can read and review it in several different ways. Everything I have to say about adventure is presented in six progressive steps:

1. Leap before You Look
2. Aim Higher Than Everest
3. Give It All You've Got
4. Work Some Magic
5. Keep on Your Bearing
6. Enjoy the View

Each step includes two chapters. The first chapter is a true-life adventure of mine that illustrates how I learned the lessons inherent in that step. The second chapter presents original interviews with other adventurers from all walks of life—with special attention paid to insights and information that are relevant to business and organizational experience. Each of these prescriptive chapters concludes with a section titled Make Your Own Adventures, which provides three hands-on exercises. These exercises will help you bridge the gap between adventure theory and practice by firsthand experimentation.

If you want to read the tales of my exploits before anything else, you can take on all the odd-numbered chapters first, then catch the even-numbered ones later. If you're the results-oriented type on the lookout for action steps, start with the even chapters. Or you can take the conventional approach of reading from the beginning to the end. However you approach this book, I hope that you finish with a sense that there's no need to buy expensive equipment or make long-distance travel arrangements before beginning your next adventure.

Your Quest Begins Now

Above all, I want to help you see that your life is a quest in the here and now. A good adventure tale sharpens our inner vision so that we can recognize the spectacular elements of our own lives. Adventure helps us enliven our way of seeing the world around us. I hope this book and its stories, strategies, and exercises will inspire you with the willingness to take a few more chances, to leap before you look, to stretch beyond the old comfort zone. Most important, I hope you will be reminded of how each of us, simply by being alive, awakens daily at another point on a profound journey. What really nurtures us is an appreciation of the ongoing adventure of a lifetime.

THE FIRST STEP

Leap before You Look

The sense of danger must not disappear:

The way is both short and steep,

However gradual it looks from here;

Look if you like, but you will have to leap.

—W. H. AUDEN

The return from Mount Don Bosco,
Southern Patagonian Ice Cap

CHAPTER 1

Mountain-Naming in Patagonia

My childhood nickname was Puffy. By age nineteen I wasn't that puffy anymore, but the psychic residue of having gone through my entire elementary and secondary school athletic career as the last guy picked still defined my sense of self. It wasn't until I discovered hiking and rock climbing in my early teens that I found a physical activity at which I excelled. Climbing, I had decided, would be the sole focus of the rest of my life.

Cowboy Steve McAndrews seemed to have chosen more ambitiously; since leaving his Texas home, his interests had ranged widely from climbing and kayaking to music, educational theory, poetry, even dance. In his wide-brimmed Stetson and ostrich-skin boots, he'd driven his pickup truck up to Big Sur to become one of the first people I knew to get Rolfed. In the wink of an eye, this shuffling, panhandle kid had transformed himself from redneck renegade to renaissance ranchero. This transcendental trailblazer was also my best buddy and climbing partner. So when McAndrews suggested the two of us organize a year-long climbing expedition, it never occurred to me to refuse.

"Come on, Salz," he'd chided. "Patagonia has mountains no one has ever climbed. You know, whoever is the first to climb a mountain gets to name it. What do you say we go down there and do a little mountain-naming?"

The conversation had begun earlier that year as we practiced our winter mountaineering skills in the mountains outside Silverton, Colorado. It had continued into the summer as we journeyed up to Crested Butte to make a few bucks teaching climbing and kayaking to high school students. Our pupils were not much younger than we were.

McAndrews, fresh off a feed lot in Hereford, Texas, was twenty years old and already a better climber than I would ever be. A few years earlier, he had traded in his lariat for a climbing rope and taken to clambering up walls of sheer granite the way he had once climbed atop Brahma bulls and bucking broncos. McAndrews wasn't much bigger than I, but he was large muscled from growing up on a working cattle ranch. He had to buy his blue jeans on the loose side just to get them over his massive upper legs. He was sandy haired and freckled, with baleful blue eyes that reflected a wisdom far beyond his years. No one who met him disliked him, nor could they quite figure him out. He was a redneck with the unaffected soulfulness of a jazz musician.

He took his time getting anywhere, loping lazily rather than walking. The first time I met him, I thought that he moved through the world far too slowly. Later, I came to see that I was the one living too fast. While I lifted life up and hurled it over my shoulder in a mad rush to experience more, McAndrews took his sweet time, examining each moment as though it were a many-faceted jewel. ("Life is precious," he said. "Why hurry a precious thing?") There was an otherworldliness about him that you didn't expect from a down-home cattleman's kid from the panhandle. And there was a tinge of sadness in his smile.

Patagonia begins where the rest of the world leaves off. At the tail end of the South American continent, it's known to have the worst weather in the world. Beginning at the barren, empty pampas of Argentina—at the line of longitude so windswept it is known as the Roaring Forties—Patagonia stretches southward toward its abrupt terminus, the icy, stormy Tierra del Fuego, often called the "uttermost part of the earth."

McAndrews had done his research. There is a place called the Southern Patagonian Ice Cap, where glaciers and wilderness extend from a series of lakes on the Argentine side all the way across to the Pacific Ocean. No one had yet traversed its width. Mountains rise up from its frozen surface: beautiful spires of ice and granite, unclimbed and unnamed. We would cross the glaciers, traverse the ice cap on skis, and climb some mountains.

Because an impressive-sounding name and official stationery were essential to solicit free gear from mountaineering equipment manufacturers and charm suspicious officials of Latin American governments, the "American Ski Mountaineering Expedition" was born. McAndrews and I recruited two college chums to round out our team. Noel Cox, mountain guide and experienced Outward Bound instructor, was the most seasoned expedition member. Her shoulder-length blond hair, mischievous grin, and diminutive stature belied her inner toughness. Just over five feet tall, she reached halfway up the chest of the fourth member of our team, Randy Udall. The son of a U.S. congressman and descendant of Mormon pioneer and outlaw John D. Lee, Randy truly seemed larger than life, from his size-twelve climbing boots to the strength of his intellect and opinions.

From Estancia Cristina—the isolated, Brigadoon-like hamlet up a wind-whipped fjord at the extreme north-northeast corner of Lago Argentina—it took a week to set up a base camp at the foot of the moving river of ice known as the Upsala Glacier. We wove through twisted strata of exposed earth—sulfuric yellows, red oxides, canyons of color carved by aeons of ice. The metal sledges lashed to our backs transformed us into offerings to the wind that threatened to lift us kitelike into the skies. When the gusts came, we clamped on to the nearest boulder and held on for dear life.

Weeks were spent scouting our route, threading the frozen labyrinth of the Upsala, the longest glacier in the Americas. Strapping on our crampons—the sharp metal spikes that climbers affix to the soles of their boots for travel over ice—we were unprepared for the fantastical frozen universe we were about to enter. Turquoise rivers, borne on an icy surface, carved heavenly grottoes and then thundered downward and disappeared into crystalline chasms thirty feet deep. Like four blind mice wearing dark glacier glasses, probing with our ice axes, we felt our way forward day after day. Roped to each other and reeling under our extreme loads, we threaded the convoluted maze of crevasses.

There were sudden screams and curses each time one of us disappeared waist-deep into potholes filled with ice water that lay concealed like booby traps beneath the slush. A week passed while we lost feeling in our toes. We tucked our boots, soggy as sponges at day's end, between sleeping bags, only to find them frozen solid each morning.

Often we stopped to marvel at the wild world that engulfed us. To endure the ceaseless insults of discomfort and insecurity that filled our days, it was essential to cultivate corresponding qualities of awe and appreciation. Slowly, grudgingly, the ice yielded its secrets: we discovered patterns within the chaos. Soon we were navigating the crystalline white caps with confidence. Hateful cul-de-sacs became the exception rather than the rule. By the end of week two, we had established marked pathways and set up glacier camp midway across the Upsala.

On the glacier at night, my dreams were of train wrecks and explosions. Our tents, pegged to the icy terrain, billowed in the angry gusts that hurtled down upon us from the north. The nylon of the tents whipped and cracked. Our lungs filled with the rush of frozen air as the tent inflated to the bursting point and seams popped with pressure. I imagined the metal screws that held our flimsy shelters to the ice tearing loose, our tents taking to the sky and heading toward the South Pole.

Life inside a Snowdrift

Thirty-five days after departing Estancia Cristina we established an advanced base camp, a snow cave feverishly dug in the face of a great tempest that bore down on us from the north. Buried ten feet deep in the snow beneath the rock towers of the ice-cap peak called Mount Murallon—the Fortress—the four of us lay hip to hip, shoulder to shoulder, shivering in a space that was the equivalent of a household refrigerator. We had no choice but to wait for the storm to pass. We waited for two weeks.

By day, time crawled slowly. The diffused light was enough to read by. At night, our cave felt like a group coffin; darkness was absolute.

As each night's blizzard deposited additional feet of snow on our hatchway, each morning's foray to the glacier for water required an additional half hour of digging to reach the surface. Once topside, you never knew what to expect. One morning, blowing winds of a hundred miles an hour dropped Randy and McAndrews to their knees, propelling them forward like a two-man luge. It took them an hour, crawling face to the snow, pulling themselves arm over arm with their ice axes, to regain the entryway.

Another morning, Noel and I emerged into total stillness. An eerie whiteout blended the horizon and sky into one seamless dream. All that was visible were the tips of our toes. All that was audible was our breathing.

Each day we sank deeper beneath the drifts. A flickering candle let us know that death by asphyxiation was not yet imminent; there was still oxygen enough to keep us alive. We bickered for lack of anything else to do. Though it was April, we sang Christmas carols through chattering teeth. I set a record in the sleeping bag competition: thirty hours elapsed without my leaving a soggy synthetic cocoon.

One week passed.

Then another.

It was McAndrews, returning from the surface with the morning weather report, who woke us from our state of suspended animation. "It's been so long that I'm not sure, but I think those tiny lights in the sky would have to be stars."

The unclimbed mountains that waited across the ice cap seemed a long, long way from where the four of us sat in the pitch-blackness pondering our next move. We had consumed much of our fuel and food while waiting for a break in the weather. Was it prudent, we wondered, to pack up our ropes, climbing metal, and already waterlogged down gear to begin skiing deeper into terra incognita?

I recounted a dream from the night before. Mickey Rooney had appeared with a truckload of cabbages for me to drive over a hill. The dream was an omen, I decided; we had to press on. Randy agreed that the dream was significant: "A sign of the mental decay that accompanies physical deterioration caused by weeks of inactivity." I knew he was right. We would have to head back across the ice, past glacier camp, and back to dry land.

But first there was a mountain to climb.

Rising above us, Mount Don Bosco, the mountain within whose flanks we had established our snow cave, had but one recorded ascent. The British explorer Eric Shipton and his team summitted in 1961 at the conclusion of a fifty-two-day trek along the ice cap. We suited up, grabbed ropes, ice screws and axes, and emerged into the starlight of the waning ice-cap night. The second ascent would be ours.

First light found us flailing waist-deep through powdery snow, breaststroking toward the East Ridge. The rising sun poked over the glacier's edge, illuminating the ice with a fire of brilliant amber. Mount Murallon, Mount Bertrand, and Mount Bertrand's equally beautiful unclimbed satellite peak glistened in ice, towering above us like quartz crystals of the gods. Atop the ridge, thin sheets of verglas crumbled into crystals, filling our path with rainbows.

Hours passed unnoticed. There were moments of grace as our axes and the front points of our crampons chomped repetitively into the vertical ice and held fast. Screws were set and ropes were threaded through carabiners with a sure, rhythmic ease. At other times our efforts degenerated into slapstick. We stood on each other's shoulders, hauling and pushing each other over collapsing snowbridges, and we floundered through new powder so deep we would never find bottom.

Unroping, moving on our own, we attained the mountain's principal ridge. None of us had ever witnessed such a sight. The entire range of glistening peaks and sheer rock pinnacles shimmered before us in the bright sun. For a moment I stood lost in amazement. Then I took a single step forward and felt the world disappear beneath my feet.

I'd made a deadly error. Fatigue combined with overconfidence had caused me to succumb to an optical illusion. Through the dark lenses of my glacier goggles, I had confused the snow beneath my boots with the whiteness beyond and had strolled blithely over the lip of the abyss! The once-gentle ridge top was now an ice cornice with a jagged edge that ended in a spectacular drop of several thousand feet.

So, it seemed, had my life. As I teetered forward, my mind filled with regret and the recrimination that must be the final thought of many soon-to-be-no-more climbers: what an idiot! Suddenly, there was a tug at my waist and I felt myself being jerked backward. Glancing over my shoulder I saw McAndrews, rope in hand, leaning back, counterbalancing my weight with his. A split second more and I'd have been on a one-way ride to oblivion. Instead, overcome with vertigo, I fell to my hands and knees on the ice.

"Thanks," I gasped.

"No problemo," nodded McAndrews, cool as ever.

Apparently my number was not up. Not yet.

The summit was in sight. We moved slowly upward along the ridge, climbing through haystacks of rime ice—freezing rain hurled with such force and at such low temperatures that it creates formations with the swirling intricacy of brain coral. McAndrews, who was at the front of the team, stopped and motioned for me to take the last lead. The final pitch was steep but not technically difficult. Securing the rope with a boot-ax belay, I guided each member of the team to within a few feet of the summit. When we were all in place, we joined hands and stepped to the top. Spontaneously, we began to sing.

My heart soared like a condor. I witnessed the planet as primordial and as fresh as the day it was born. Thousands of square miles of virgin earth surrounded us, uncharted, untrammeled, and unknown. Directly below us, the Upsala Glacier extended forty frozen miles before turning into icebergs and disappearing into Lago Argentino. One hundred miles to the north we could see the legendary monolith of Mount FitzRoy, its mile of solid granite gleaming purple, its silhouette like a spaceship heading skyward. Someday, I said to myself, we'll do FitzRoy.

You never conquer a mountain. If you make the summit, all you have conquered is yourself. There, on that peak, we gained the upper hand on our fears, our self-doubts, our own inner inertia. On the mountaintop we felt our souls expanding and prayed that some part of this newfound largesse of spirit would linger forever.

Eight days later we stepped once more upon the living earth. The loam felt deliciously spongy beneath my feet. I was overwhelmed by the texture of the leaves, the colors of the flowers. After weeks of near-total sensory deprivation, we had emerged from a frozen moonscape into the Garden of Eden. I dug my fingers into the earth and burrowed my face into a soft patch of moss. Lustily, I sucked in the sweet smell of life.

CHAPTER 2

Make Your Leap
of Faith

Successful people are seldom purely outcome-oriented; they delight equally in the process and the result. Surprisingly, their insistence on immediate gratification, on savoring the intrinsic pleasures of each moment, turns out to be the most effective method for dealing with the vicissitudes of long-term change.

If we always do what we've always done, we'll always get what we've always gotten. The only thing about which we can be certain is that today's solution will no longer work tomorrow. We rekindle our love affair with life and improve our chances of success every time we try something we have never tried and go someplace we have never been.

Innovation Requires Action

As a speaker and consultant working with some of America's most dynamic executives and corporations over the last few years, I have discovered one fundamental truth: Successful individuals and organizations innovate; radically successful individuals and organizations innovate radically. To take first prize requires taking a chance. When we are innovative, we don't always have the luxury of waiting for all the information to be in because, quite simply, the information is never all in.

Innovation means action. When crossing a busy street, we cannot look both ways at the same time. We look one way, then the other. We assess the situation, calculate the odds, and make necessary preparations. But then we must leap. Gathering our gumption, we put pedal to the metal and make our move. Or we will never go anywhere at all.

In much the same way, the pace of today's world no longer permits us the luxury of prolonged deliberation. We must grow comfortable taking action before all the data is compiled, neatly graphed, and pie-charted; before all the subcommittees and focus groups have made their reports. We must be willing to find our courage, gather our wits, trust our instincts, and take the leap—sometimes before we look.

Begin with the End

"To me, leaping means always starting with the ending I want," says Norm Fawley, self-educated inventor and president of NCF Industries. Norm holds more than twenty-five patents and is a leading developer of composite materials (like fiberglass-reinforced plastic) that do everything from increasing the strength of highway bridge supports to decreasing the weight of oxygen cylinders used by high-altitude climbers. Norm's light-weight air cylinders helped make possible the first American ascent of Mount Everest. "I always begin with the conviction that the thing will work even before I start to make it. I don't just postulate a hypothesis about something that is supposed to work. I physically go do it!"

Norm and I first became friends on a Himalayan expedition I was leading in western Nepal close to the Tibetan border. One afternoon in particular cemented our friendship. After several days of rigorous climbing, I realized I had lost track of something important: our location. We were heading for a settlement previously unvisited by Westerners, rumored to be an inspiration for the legend of Shangri-la. We had spent most of the day struggling through knee-deep snow, heading toward a pass through the mountains. Our lucky break came almost at dusk when, as if from nowhere, a party of yak herders carrying salt from Tibet appeared above us, thundering by with a flurry of greetings and hooves. For several hours we were able to follow the trail they had left behind. I informed Norm and the rest of my party that we would camp just a few minutes beyond the pass. There were cheers, especially from Norm, whose knee injury was acting up painfully. Darkness was almost upon us when we topped the rocky outcropping and found ourselves gazing down a precipitous ice gully several thousand feet long. Suddenly the possibility of finding a warm, dry, flat camp was very remote.

As we pulled together to survive this and other fiascoes that followed, Norm and I became fast friends. Over the course of many tent-bound evenings and pots of Sherpa potato stew, I learned a lot from this freewheeling, wildly successful inventor.

"Whenever I get the feeling that what I am doing is right, I just do it," says Norm.

In our modern-day society, so many people have lost the belief in their innate capacities. They plan too much, and then they slip into what I call paralysis through analysis. They go through life wanting to do something, but not believing they ever will. Ten thousand years ago, you didn't sit at a fork in the road and wait for someone to bring you a map and a weather forecast. Hannibal crossed the Alps, Magellan sailed the world and somebody irrigated Chaco Canyon. How did people get such things done? Not by sticking a toe in the water and waiting for it to warm up. They leaped.

You Always Know What to Do

Norm and I later spent some time together in eastern Nepal, close to the Tibetan border. When we once had the opportunity to seek advice from the local high lama at a mountaintop monastery, Norm spoke out. "Everybody was asking the lama, 'What should I do with my life?' What popped into my head was, 'What can I do for your village?' That threw the lama for a loop; he didn't know what to say. After a while, he came back and told me, 'You always know what to do.' Now I was thrown for a loop! This was a very perplexing piece of information for me at that time. But it has turned out to be true ever since."

What Norm did for the Nepalese was to bring corn, squash, and sunflower seeds back from his ranch in southern California on subsequent expeditions. In the last few years I have seen stands of giant sunflowers towering up over fences in tiny villages far from Kathmandu. I have eaten their seeds, toasted and salted, along with potato stews containing huge hunks of sweet yellow squash. One day I asked my Nepali host where he had obtained such tasty and unusually large squash.

He shrugged his shoulders. "Somebody came through," was his reply.

Making a difference does not depend on intellect alone. Coming up with an idea is only the beginning; it is "coming through" with action that completes the equation. While ideas are necessary to plot the course, action alone hoists the anchor and sets sail for success. We may always know what to do, as the lama told Norm, but in doing it lies the thrill of adventure.

Our creativity, innate wisdom, and capacity for greatness always lie just below the surface, awaiting the moment we pick up the pen, grab the brush, or attack the keyboard. "Whatever you can do, or dream you can do, begin it. Boldness has genius power and magic in it," wrote Goethe. Whether we are taking on a new job or creating our own, beginning a new relationship or revitalizing an old one, if we trust in our own capabilities we will seldom be disappointed. The only guarantee of disappointment is never to leap at all.

Look for "Inventure"

I asked my friend Dick Leider why more people don't take leaps of vision. According to Dick, the urge to explore—which comes easily to us in our early years—fades soon after college for the simple reason that we get out of the habit. Dick has spent a lifetime in career counseling and now runs a consulting firm called the Inventure Group. He's an experienced outdoorsman who has written a number of popular books on attaining personal and business success. Nowadays, Dick works most often with senior executives in major corporations; that is, when he is not on yearly expeditions to Africa, where he was recently initiated as an elder in the Masai tribe. Here's what Dick has to say about keeping one's sense of adventure alive:

> We can spend so much of our lives, especially in corporate environments, cogitating and contemplating without actually experimenting, experiencing firsthand, and taking risks. In the first half of life, you may get a good game going in conventional terms of salary, and then before you know it, your life has become a replication of the same old patterns leading to numbness. I meet a lot of people who are highly successful but feel numb and unfulfilled. This is because they have defined success only in an external, power-and-money way. Not that I am against power and money, but we all discover sooner or later that it is not everything in life.
>
> I see more and more people approaching the second half of life with something new uppermost in their minds. They

are looking for the rest of themselves. They have played by the external rules for so long, they don't know how to go inside themselves and find what is missing. They fear the inventure—the risky journey into their own unknown territory.

Change Your Environment

In our roles as expedition leaders, Dick and I have both experienced the truth of the old Outward Bound dictum: we become more alive simply by changing our environments—particularly by entering the wild. In a novel setting where we can no longer count on things being as they were, our senses become more finely attuned and our instincts sharpen. Leaping into an unfamiliar environment—be it a trip to the other side of town or the other side of the world—is a sure ticket to a revitalized awareness.

"People feel much more alive on a trek and then they want to know how to bottle that experience and bring it back home with them," Dick comments. "And they hunger to share what they felt. For a while they may stay in touch with other trekkers they met, but eventually the experience recedes if they don't do something to keep it alive in their everyday environment."

And how do we keep that spirit of adventure alive in everyday life? Try creating your own personal *inventures*. "Everyone is an experiment of one," Dick says, "and what to do depends on your environment and personal issues." But he agrees that an effective first step is to change your internal environment—that is, to pursue on a regular basis some creative expression or activity that is uncomfortable or unfamiliar to you, and see where it takes you. When you launch yourself into new internal territory, sometimes you will fail miserably—but you have already succeeded! Because regardless of the outcome, you feel more alive.

The real reason to leap before you look is that after the split second of initial discomfort, your entire being starts to feel so good. Your adrenaline pumps, your pulse quickens, your breath grows short, your eyes open, and your nostrils flare wide. As your feet leave solid ground, even momentarily, you rediscover your own aliveness and find yourself renewed, revitalized, and awakened.

Take a Flying Leap

My colleague Jim McCormick, an M.B.A. who once served as the chief operating officer of an international architectural firm and now works for himself as a motivational speaker and consultant, often raises eyebrows—not to mention pulses—when he greets a new client. That's because Jim has a penchant for leaping out of the sky trailing an American flag and a trail of smoke, then landing within a stone's throw of his astonished clientele.

A world-record holder and North Pole sky diver who advertises himself as a leading authority on risk taking, Jim showed up for the first meeting with his publisher after taking such a flying leap, and he has staged similarly vivid demonstrations of risk for such clients as Hewlett-Packard, Bank of America, Sun Microsystems, and the American Payroll Association. Jim explains, "You have only one chance to make an unforgettable first impression."

Trust Your Instincts over Information

Jim is teaching a deeper lesson than showmanship to today's corporate movers and thinkers. "Today's businesspeople have to trust their instincts more than ever before," he muses. "Things are happening so quickly that they can't go to the same level of study and preparation that used to be possible. I interviewed a fellow who started up two Silicon Valley firms who said that the greatest challenge he faced as an executive was having to make decisions on what he knew was insufficient information. Because he knew that if he waited until all the information was in, the opportunity at hand would pass him by."

That's where Jim makes the connection between skydiving and the modern business climate:

People always ask if I was scared for my first jump, and I say of course. And I'm still scared, because every time I leave the plane I'm potentially killing myself. In that situation, some degree of fear is healthy! What's relevant for businesspeople to understand is that if I wanted to be totally prepared for every possibility, I would never have made my first jump. You don't have to be particularly imaginative to come up with a fatal scenario, and it does happen to people on their first jumps. But if I was overly concerned about that, I would never have proceeded.

Again and again I've heard stories of companies in the midst of rapidly reshaping their approach—whether they're expanding, downsizing, or changing their market position—having to tell their people, The old ways don't work anymore and we have no way of knowing if the new way we've chosen will work. But we have no choice but to go ahead. No one has the luxury of defending the status quo any longer, partly because the competition is now coming not only from new contenders in the same field but from whole new forms of commerce that didn't even exist a few years ago.

Engage in Risky Business

Jim's point seems almost understated when you reflect that such major players in the current American economy as Amazon.com or America Online not only didn't exist ten years ago, they weren't even being imagined. The Internet itself, perhaps the most significant force in the rapid reshaping of worldwide marketing, was not in the public view until 1994 and was just beginning to gain popularity by 1996.

Jim adds that the capacity to engage in "risky business" is crucial for individuals as well as companies:

> One thing that's so exciting about today's business world is that losing your job is no longer a badge of shame. In fact it's inevitable. The single-employer career is history, and the single-occupation career is on the way out, too. That means people need to take risks in their careers in order to advance. Even the risk-averse type who likes to play it safe is going to get fired. It's the corporate adventurers who not only land on their feet but end up at the top of organizations—or heading up their own companies. That's why I teach the importance of lifetime education. People must be retraining themselves on a perpetual basis. But in the final analysis, whether you're on the high-speed train to the future or just watching it go by depends chiefly on how comfortable you are taking risks.

Go for Maximum Aliveness

Joseph Campbell, the scholar of mythology and philosophy, came to the conclusion that maximum aliveness is the ultimate prize. "People say we are seeking a meaning for life. I don't think that is really what we are seeking. What we are seeking is to feel the rapture of being alive."

In his book *The Hero of a Thousand Faces*, Campbell offers us a schematic of the archetypal hero's journey—a topographical map of the elevated terrain of the human spirit. This map is, far and away, the best navigational chart I can recommend for the trip. And Joseph Campbell is among the finest guides I have encountered. An archaeologist of the human story, Campbell has traveled the world sifting through our species' subconscious and digging up a template that transcends time and culture. His work provides a blueprint by which to construct a meaningful life and a resource to consult when the trek toward a goal seems to be getting off course. It is the map that all adventurers of the spirit will do well to keep on hand for easy and frequent reference on the circuitous path ahead.

Campbell believes that the basic storyline of the human experience has remained unchanged from the stories of Gilgamesh of Mesopotamia and King Arthur of ancient Britain to modern-day movie epics like the *Star Wars* trilogy (for which his research served as inspiration). We would do well to recognize it as our story, too. According to Campbell, "A hero ventures forth from the world of common day into a region of supernatural wonder: fabulous forces are there encountered and a decisive victory is won: the hero comes back from this mysterious adventure with the power to bestow boons on his fellow man."

For all of us, the initial step is always a leap—of faith.

The Stages and Gifts of the Journey

A herald appears to instigate our journey. The herald is the individual or experience that delivers the wake-up call, challenging and inviting us to leave the comfort of familiar shores behind—just as Steve McAndrews called to me to head for Patagonia. To answer that call requires a level of trust and a willingness to fly by instinct and the seat of our pants. There is rough and unfamiliar country ahead, adversity and uncertainty. We must remember that the night always looks darkest—just before it goes totally black. Then we hit bottom.

Every quest must have a Dark Night of the Soul, its Pit of Despair. Losing our orientation, we may feel totally defeated.

But we can remain in the pit for only so long. Life's natural buoyancy reasserts itself and we find ourselves lifted upward once again toward the light. At last we experience some success. We vanquish a couple of dragons and begin to realize the three principal gifts of our subterranean odyssey:

1. We have gained a heartier faith in life than we had heretofore known.

2. We acknowledge that we have the power to make a significant difference in the circumstances of our lives and the world around us.

3. We discover that along the way we have forged new and profound alliances, not only with individuals but with our own humanity.

It's the Doing That Makes the Being

We must all leap wholeheartedly into everyday life; we must commit ourselves daily to move in the direction of our dreams. If we are to make measurable progress we must define ourselves in deeds, not just words. The human doing creates the human being. With equal parts audacity and uncertainty, we take the plunge. Surprised at the sound of our voice saying yes, the sight of our hand raising to volunteer, we find ourselves stretching toward what we hoped we might become. Playing for higher stakes we master the game more quickly.

"I can't say that I love danger," wrote André Gide, "but I love a life of risk. I want life to demand of me, at every moment, all of my courage, all of my happiness, all of my health." Life is the ultimate Olympiad. We qualify at birth. Sometime later the herald arrives, the starting gun sounds, and—if we choose to answer the call—the event begins.

For a kid from Jersey, my journey to Patagonia was a real-life Alice in Wonderland experience. I had gained entry into a world of adventure and freedom that I had only imagined before—a country of marvels to which, despite its dicey moments, I would always return. My first visit to South America changed me forever. Having stepped through the looking glass, I had begun my hero's journey and would never look back. How could I have known that the leaping was the easy part and that the most difficult moments of my life lay just a few months ahead?

Make Your Own Adventures

When daily life has begun to fit you like a cheap suit—constricting here, chafing there— it's time for a radical alteration. Vicarious adventuring won't induce the kind of changes your spirit craves. So let's do something to make "leaping before you look" a reality in your own life. Although I won't be recommending anything that's truly dangerous, you should be aware that all true adventure entails some degree of risk. It's up to you to choose the kind of undertaking and level of difficulty that you're willing to attempt. In any case, remember that it's more important to challenge your internal limits of daring than your physical limits or capacities.

I'll start you off easy. Here are three kinds of "leaps" you can try without looking—and without quitting your job, investing in expensive equipment, or risking anything besides your complacency.

1. GET OFF TO A FAST START

This one is almost too easy. But you'll quickly learn how your inner life can be altered by a simple change in your external circumstances:

Spend a day fasting from something you usually depend on to get you through the day.

The object of your fast can be a particular food or beverage, cigarettes, happy hour, television, even your car. The art of transforming hardship into a successful adventure requires learning to do without in order to go within.

The greatest benefit of survival training—a contrived discipline that teaches one how to light a fire without matches, find food by scrounging from the natural landscape with only a pocketknife for a weapon, and cross scary chasms without a toll bridge—is not that we will be able to last through the next world war or Internet glitch. Any good wilderness survival course will teach you that your strength and resourcefulness depend on knowing just how little you really need. Despite the constant bombardment of advertising that tries to convince us otherwise, most of us could indeed get by with next to nothing if we had to. And it's precisely that awareness that reawakens our slumbering spirit and restores us to a natural condition of robust tenacity—the ability to laugh and reorganize our priorities in case the Dow drops a few hundred points, or we run out of gas seventy miles from the nearest station, or we find ourselves stuck in Lagos, Nigeria, for a week longer than planned, without a hotel or credit card. With the adventuring spirit that finds challenge in deprivation, we can plumb our resolve, access our inner resources, and somehow find a way to get by.

Occasional fasting in the midst of your everyday life keeps your inner resourcefulness honed and available for access. Make sure you fast from something you will notice, but don't turn it into self-punishment. Watch yourself get edgy from not doing what you usually do, but don't give in to the urge to return to normal. To be on the edge is to be on the frontier of adventure. When you discover that your sense of well-being doesn't have to be tied to a familiar commodity or comfort, you will be getting a taste of the adventurer's freedom—the intense aliveness that derives from leaping before you look.

2. LIVE FOR FORTY-EIGHT ON FIFTY

This advanced version of the preceding exercise couldn't be simpler, but it is guaranteed to jolt you out of your ordinary ways of getting through the day:

> Spend forty-eight hours away from home on fifty cents or less.

Though this was the template for my earliest adventure, I wouldn't necessarily recommend doing this for other kids. As a child growing up in New Jersey, long before I discovered the natural world I explored the wilderness at my doorstep: New York City. Having convinced my parents that I was off to a bar mitzvah or a sleep-away party, I would ride the #77 bus into the city, armed only with the change in my pocket. I wanted to see what the world looked like outside suburbia; it was an eye-opener, to say the least. I slept on benches in Central Park and Penn Station until cops woke me with a nightstick in the ribs. I felt the hopeless rejection of seeing every door—to restaurants, movie theaters, convenience stores—no longer open or off-limits to a kid without any money. My fourteen-year-old soul got an intimation of what it was like to be homeless or impoverished, an experience that my caring parents certainly wouldn't have arranged for me!

Later, when I was seventeen, I carried out sort of a dry run for all the adventures that would follow in my life. I spent three nights living in the Disneyland jungle at Anaheim. I didn't break any rules; I even paid full price to get in. But I didn't bother to leave when everyone else did. Instead, I climbed over a wall between the Swiss Family Robinson treehouse and the Pirates of the Caribbean ride, then bedded down between the mechanical gazelles and the animated rhino. I spent no money, stole nothing, and lived on Space Food Sticks while prowling the park. When they apprehended me on the third night, the security guards informed me that they had been after "the jungle man" for two days and hospitably escorted me off the property. Years later, when I had become a university professor, I would hear from students working summer jobs at Disneyland that "the Jungleman from Jersey" was still a part of the park's lore.

The moral of the story is the preview for your own fund-free expedition: The less you spend, the more you experience! The safety cushion we call money often insulates us from a more intense and invigorating reality.

3. BECOME AN ALIEN

Adventure is a sink-or-swim initiation; your learning curve accelerates dramatically as soon as you take the plunge. Nothing can replace uncertainty as a catalyst for growth. You can create initiations in your professional life this way:

Go undercover in another department or even another company than your own.

As a guest speaker and trainer, I get this opportunity frequently. I show up at a work site or convention prior to my own engagement in order to scope out the group. My host and I keep my identity a secret. Suddenly I am sitting in on the board meeting, eating tiny hot dogs at the cocktail party, or doing the meringue as a mystery guest—not honorary or special, just unidentified. It's amazing how much I can learn about an organization's behavior, and my own, when I am stripped of my professional persona even for a short time. You can try it, too. Sell the idea to your boss or supervisor as an educational experience; maybe someone in another department or business can take your place as well. Just introduce yourself as a "consultant" from the ABCDE Corporation for the length of a project meeting, cocktail party, or convention session.

Disclaimer: This exercise is *not* an invitation to conduct industrial espionage! As an adventurer your aim is to enliven your inner life, not to run an intelligence operation.

Whenever you can find a way to leap at work, expanding beyond your usual pigeonhole or accustomed sphere of expertise, your professional world grows larger, and more often than not, your enthusiasm will be noted. I have heard many an executive complain about employees who are unwilling to venture beyond their comfort zones, take chances, or use their imagination to enhance everyone's productivity or quality of work life. I have never heard employees criticized for being too daring or innovative. You can "become an alien" with a very small step, if you wish—just try a new water-cooler clique down the hall or on another floor and progress from there. Later, try volunteering for a team task in which you have no expertise and see what kind of adventure follows. When you leap into new environments you always come out ahead, even if you don't know where you're headed.

Aim Higher Than Everest

In the long run men hit only what they aim at.

Therefore, though they should fail immediately,

They had better aim at something high.

—HENRY DAVID THOREAU

Steve McAndrews ascending the Super Couloir,
Mount FitzRoy, Argentina

CHAPTER 3

The Freaker's Ball
Expedition

McAndrews and I had shared quite a year. In April, after the ice cap experience, Randy and Noel had undertaken the weeklong cross-country hike out from Estancia Cristina. They'd chanced upon a dirt road, stuck out their thumbs, and within a couple of days were safely back in Calafate, the true capital of Argentine Patagonia. McAndrews and I, however, had opted for what seemed to be the easier escape route. We figured we would wait a couple of weeks on the far side of Lago Argentino with our crates of expedition supplies as guests of Estancia Cristina and its eccentric British patron, Bert Masters. "I'll be sending the boat out any day now," he swore.

April passed. Suddenly May, too, was gone. By June we realized that because he didn't receive many guests, Bert Masters was in no hurry to see us leave. "We'll be taking the boat out any month now," he said. In desperation, we tried to hike out, leaving our gear behind. We were forced to turn around when we were apprehended by a blizzard. In July we got tired of climbing the walls and decided to head for the hills instead. We crossed the Upsala Glacier in two days. On the third day we made it halfway up an unclimbed peak before an ice wall turned us back.

On the fourth, in one massive effort, we made it all the way back to the estancia, empty-handed but happy.

Finally, in August, just when parents and friends back in the States had begun organizing a search party, a government boat showed up to ask Bert Masters why he never paid taxes. McAndrews and I jumped aboard and made our escape. By September, we'd landed in Chile amid the political fireworks that toppled the socialist government of Salvador Allende and replaced it with the tyrannical rule of Pinochet. In October, McAndrews and I managed to squeeze in a few climbs in the Peruvian Andes, including the first ascent or two in the Cordillera Urubamba. A rented adobe in the town of Urubamba had served as our clubhouse while the team formed, catalyzed by the notion of scaling Mount FitzRoy.

Beyond the windswept badlands populated only by ostrich, fox, guanaco, sheep, and the humble outposts of the gauchos, the solitary monolith loomed among the clouds. With its mile-long face of vertical rock relentlessly whipped by the wind, its sides scoured by avalanches, FitzRoy had long been a legend. Charles Darwin, the great naturalist aboard the HMS *Beagle*, had sighted it in 1834. He was so awestruck by the immensity of the obelisk that rose in grandeur from the flats that he named it in honor of the ship's captain. FitzRoy's dramatic location on the edge of the ice cap, as well as its startling size, has awed visitors ever since. For mountaineers, the mountain's five-thousand-foot sheer walls of orange granite soon became a kind of Holy Grail.

For young climbers like us, a successful ascent of FitzRoy would be a rite of passage; its summit would be the ultimate trophy. Seasoned and fit from a summer of climbing in the Andes of Peru, we were ready to take on the big one. Almost.

"*Ay, Dios,* but the legend!" worried our friend and hotelier Rosa when she learned why we had returned to Patagonia. "The local Indians say that when the cloud covers the mountain it is the evil spirits. If the cloud finds you it will be terrible tragedy."

"I promise you, señora, we will not climb if it gets too cloudy. Too hard to see, anyway," McAndrews assured her.

It was October, almost a year since we had arrived on foot and full of idealism in Argentina. Now Noel popped an Elton John cassette into the tape deck of the shiny pickup that stuck out like a lunar module in the dusty lot in front of doña Rosa's ramshackle hotel. Noel's many months of travel in developing countries had transformed her into a savvy and confident road warrior. A little high-altitude romance hadn't done her self-esteem any harm, either. In Peru, she had hooked up with David Kilcullen, a bearded New Zealand climber whose shambling appearance was at odds with his reputation as one of the top young climbers in the world. We all fell for David the day Noel brought him home to meet us, her second family.

David's best friend, Kevin Carrol, had also joined our ragtag band. With his shaggy Prince Valiant haircut falling onto broad shoulders, Kevin was a unique mix of hulking mountaineer and awkward schoolboy. He had recently drawn the attention of the international mountaineering community by pulling off the first ascent of the Caroline Face of Mount Cook, the most difficult and dangerous route up the highest summit in New Zealand. Kevin's entire existence was climbing. He admitted to having a hard time communicating with "flatlanders"; only in the heights did he feel at home. "I grew up in the mountains," I heard him explain one day in his heavy Kiwi burr. "I've lived in the mountains, and if I'm lucky, by God, someday I'll die and be buried in the mountains."

We had officially rebaptized ourselves the American/New Zealand Andean Expedition. Less reverently we called ourselves "The Freaker's Ball" after our favorite Dr. Hook and the Medicine Show tune:

Blow your whistle, bang your gong
Roll up something to take along
It feels so good, it must be wrong
Freakin' at the Freaker's Ball

Our climbing hardware—pitons, nuts, and ice screws—was threaded on electric lime green and flaming flamingo pink perlon marked with the words "Freaker's Ball Expedition."

The days spent at doña Rosa's in final preparation were full of laughter and smart remarks. Of course, this was a case of excessive bravado rooted in uncertainty. At night we could hardly sleep. We tossed and turned, unnerved to the core by the magnitude of our dreams. In one long, bone-jouncing day, we traveled by pickup from Calafate to the end of the rutted road. Sleeping bags were laid down beneath dreary skies. In the morning we tottered sleepily from the warmth of our bags and stood gazing at the massive towers of the FitzRoy range suddenly revealed against a miraculously clear sky.

It required several trips to stock our base camp for the six weeks we anticipated it would take for the climb. Our route was across lush meadows of yellow wildflowers, through waist-deep icy rivers, and into dense forests of linga trees and shadows. All the while reigning above us was FitzRoy. For any mountaineer this was the Big Time. I carried my load, carefully watching my feet. I dared not look up. I knew FitzRoy would be staring me down.

Expeditions don't qualify as the most relaxing getaway vacations. It took a day and a half to reach the shanty that was to be our base camp. Along the way I felt like a human offering to the wind, spinning like a top, breathlessly careening sideways along glacial moraines. More than once, I was backhanded by sudden gusts into a river, and emerged exhausted, frozen, and trembling.

We carried loads like this, nonstop, for three days. Every day, all day, until the last load was finally delivered. McAndrews and Kevin headed up into the glacier to dig a snow cave at the base of the west side of FitzRoy beneath our route: the Super Couloir.

It was to be Kevin, Dave, McAndrews, and me on the climb— New Zealand and American teams, two ropes of two, climbing alpine style. Noel sorted food, fuel, and climbing gear. She would remain on-site, as support. The morning after base camp was finally stocked, Randy and his friend Bill Martin, who had come down to be a support person for the expedition, went fishing. Having carried heavier loads than anyone else, they deserved a break. Like the rest of us, they anticipated a long delay before the action began. Well supplied, we were prepared to wait as long as a month and a half for a break in the weather.

Much to our surprise, the next morning dawned clear and cloudless. McAndrews and I ate our oatmeal in the dark and were off. Having just returned from an exploratory foray to the base of the climb, McAndrews guided us, unroped, through the canyons and ice fields of the approach. McAndrews spent much of the day shouting encouragement, reminding me that we had to take advantage of the good weather. I plodded slowly along. Still tired from the forced marches of the previous days, I couldn't go any faster.

Now I stood beneath the Super Couloir. The route was so foreshortened I did not believe that we were beneath it. Having left base camp around nine, David and Kevin, with Noel in support, were a few hours behind us. The day remained perfectly calm, not a breath of wind from the ice cap. We chose gear and began the climb. At nine-thirty, in the last glow of daylight, we were still plugging away in the soft snow. The others appeared below. "A piece of duff!" I yelled in my best Kiwi accent. The climb seemed deceptively easy, the summit seemingly within our grasp.

McAndrews smiled and said nothing.

With numb fingers, I hauled myself up to the bivouac ledge that would be our home for the night. We stepped about like landscapers, surveying our sloping chunk of rock. No spot was level or comfortable. Nonetheless, we hammered a piton into a flaring crack and anchored in. Huddled in our parkas, we ate dinner, which consisted of a chunk of cheese, crackers, and some Kool-Aid.

Sleep was a patchwork of uneasy dreams and fitful naps. With interminable slowness, the night gave way to the first rays of dawn. From our perch I could see David and Kevin starting out. My boots, foolishly placed too far away to be warmed by my body heat, had frozen solid. They thawed slowly in the morning, thudding into the hard ice as I made my way up the first few pitches.

Alternating leads, we front-pointed up a section of frozen waterfall, pounded in a screw, threaded the rope, and hacked a new belay platform in the ice. The belay consisted of a rope wrapped around our bodies, held firmly in case the second climber should fall. Between the activity and the adrenaline, hours passed like minutes. With no time to dwell on hunger and fatigue, we operated in a state beyond the physical, absorbed in a dream.

Above the ice, the first hundred feet of rock turned out to be a series of awkward cracks. McAndrews led each of these navigations in succession. I followed, jamming boots and fingertips, hips and elbows in steady, rhythmic progress. Dave and Kevin were working their way up toward us, so we left the rope hanging and suspended everything, including ourselves, for lunch. By afternoon, the two Kiwis had joined us, and McAndrews was leading for all four of us. I inched ingloriously up the rope behind him, carrying the pack and cleaning the protecting pins, nuts, and screws from the rock.

I felt like I should be doing more leading. Seconding is not really climbing, I thought. But McAndrews was smoother at this than I would ever be and speed was essential.

Dehydration and thirst set in. Pressing blistered lips to the thawing ice, I sucked in only enough to increase my desire for water. As I ascended the rope, the rough granite tore at my knuckles till they bled. Soon we were climbing in darkness, hunting unsuccessfully for a bivouac ledge. Unable to continue, we settled upon two steeply pitched shelves that tilted downward like fun-house steps.

I was exhausted, but the wall rose relentlessly before me. There was no place to rest, sit, or lie down. I grew dizzy, battling a growing insecurity. Finally, I retreated into myself; the feeling I had been fighting for days took advantage of my weakness. It took me a moment to recognize it. I never thought it would happen, but I was scared to death.

"You know something?" McAndrews tapped me on the shoulder. His voice was weak. "I've got to admit I'm kinda tired. I could use a little bit of help tonight." He had to be even more spent than I was, having taken every lead so far on the rock. I loaned McAndrews my parka while David and Kevin hauled up his pack. But the pack jammed tightly; it was wedged somewhere far below and wouldn't budge. No one volunteered to retrieve it. Hanging from the cliff face, messing around with technical climbing gear in the dark, way past exhaustion, was an invitation for tragedy.

"Hey, Steve. No worries. I'll go down and get it," I said. Rappelling into the darkness, I implored a weary brain to keep cranking for a few more stressful minutes. Descending until I was just a few feet to the side of the jammed pack, I tied a prusik knot into the rope and hitched it tight, clipped it to my waist harness, and pendulummed in the blackness. After several tries, one hand managed to reach hold of a shoulder strap. Then came the moment of truth. Entrusting my life to my equipment, I held my breath and let go. The rope tightened and held. With two hands, I heaved on the pack with all my strength. It came free and I struggled back up the rope. Now I had done more than pull pitons: I had pulled my weight.

When we believe that every ounce of energy has been wrung from our bodies, there is always something left. The mountain teaches you this: dig deeply into your soul and you will never come up empty-handed. The greatest gift given us by extreme circumstances is the opportunity to plumb our own depths and discover resources more vast than we ever imagined.

I handed the pack to McAndrews. For the first time since the climb had commenced, I was glad to be thousands of feet in the air. My presence had been crucial.

"Thanks, pardner," he said.

Day three. The good news: our warm weather seemed to be continuing. The bad news: the bright sun was thawing the frozen waterfall that had been our ticket upward. The small rocks that had been whizzing by were now replaced by boulders roaring past us. We wondered if we had strayed off-route. Easy-looking pitches had begun to end up as overhangs where hand- and footholds were nonexistent. Instead of clambering up the rock, we were spending long hours hanging from nylon slings that were threaded through the hardware we had placed in narrow vertical cracks.

With frozen feet and aching muscles, I led the first pitch of the morning. Alas, two nights out had had a debilitating effect on my ability to function. My flexibility was shot; I could barely hold my weight with my arms. We proceeded slowly and managed to complete only a few rope lengths the entire day. At day's end we appeared to be only a couple of pitches from the summit ridge and easier climbing, but we were dangerously low on food and fuel. Time was sneaking by us. From the ice cap a storm approached. We jammed ourselves together for yet another night.

We do not script the story of our lives alone. Aiming high, we enter a cocreative process with forces far larger than ourselves. Whether we call our adventure a vision quest, a pilgrimage, or a mountain climb, it is these rare moments that the universe speaks as a voice from within. If we are fortunate we may glean enough inspiration and wisdom to last a lifetime. That night, wedged between a rock and a billion stars, I got lucky.

Snow pattered upon our parkas as a cloud engulfed our ledge. Eyes wide open, I stayed awake, my bottom jammed into a fissure in the granite. The loop of rope around my waist connected me to the common sling from which we all hung. By now McAndrews's weight was crushing my loins. But I said nothing on the off chance that he might have managed to find a few precious minutes of sleep.

Suddenly I saw a home, wife, and family awaiting me below. I saw years of important work ahead and many tales to tell. I knew there was nothing for me farther up the rock. With certainty and a measure of sorrow, I realized that my path was no longer upward: I would not be the one to stand atop this summit. In my mind's eye, I could already see myself descending.

Sometime during the endless night, I suggested what had been thus far unthinkable: we could not continue to climb as we had with any hope of success. Only two should go on. Two could carry all the remaining provisions and make the top in a day, much faster than all four of us.

Shortly before dawn it was agreed. For the Americans, it would be McAndrews. He deserved it. He had climbed harder and better than any of us. Kevin would ascend for the New Zealanders. The two would finish the climb for the entire team—for Randy,

Bill, and Noel down below as well. If any one of us managed to stand atop FitzRoy, the success would belong to all of us.

Early in the morning I placed the first pin, and David and I began our descent. To our chagrin, we had come close enough to the summit that when the sun broke through, it was nearly unbearable to keep heading downward. It grew easier when the clouds rolled in and the rocks above us vanished in the mist. Rappel followed rappel, one after another. My mind grew as worn as the fraying rope in my hands as David and I struggled to remember how to tie the knots.

Most climbing accidents happen on the descent. Over and over, the rope had to be hauled down, coils made and thrown. My waist harness was unclipped from the anchor and reclipped into the confusing five-carabiner descent system. Inevitably, halfway down the rope I would find myself cursing at the knots, gnarled and jammed in seemingly malicious ways. At the end of the rope, I would tie on and swing about in search of the next piton placement. Clipping into the anchor, feeling it hold my weight, meant we had successfully descended another 150 feet without falling to our deaths. "Okay, David!" I yelled, and the whole damned business would begin again.

It was not unusual for one of us to lapse into momentary amnesia, completely losing track of the procedure and capable only of following orders. After twenty full-length rappels of 150 feet, we lost count. Although the weather had remained mild, the storm undelivered, the Super Couloir had become a river. Now the carabiner system wrung the rope dry during each rappel, pouring water into my crotch and jolting me back to alertness. Amazingly, every pin, nut, and screw held perfectly. Not a thought was wasted on the hundreds of dollars of equipment we left behind. Life was all we valued.

The rope was nearly worn through when the final rappel set us on top of the soft snow in the lower reaches of the Couloir.

We wrapped the rope around our boots and ice axes, belaying each other downward, battling to find our balance on slippery slush. Two figures awaited below on the glacier. Glissading and running, David and I leaped in unison. On waterlogged bottoms we tobogganed madly down the slope, plowing up great masses of snow between our legs. Yee-haaa! I tottered into Randy's waiting arms. Bill was there, too, with candy and peanuts. I howled as the salt attacked my snow-burned mouth.

I drifted through the next day, wholly at peace. The weather was superb. Sitting quietly by the river in the bright sunshine, my body, battered and aching, felt alive in every pore. I was awake, relaxed, and totally content. McAndrews and Kevin must be well into the descent by now, I reckoned. We had succeeded. What a glorious thing! What a wonderful life!

That night the sky filled with wind and rain. I slept a bit and dreamed of McAndrews and Kevin out in bad weather. In my nightmare, FitzRoy assumed monstrous dimensions. I woke up in a sweat, clutching my sleeping bag around me, thinking of doña Rosa and her recounting of the old Tchuelche legend.

The next morning, we returned up the glacier, scouring the mountain for signs of McAndrews and Kevin. Nothing. Our team was forced to entrench in the snow cave for another night, sleepless and worried.

At dawn we found their bodies at the foot of the climb. They had fallen a long way. Steve and Kevin were dead.

I was stunned. I felt like I had been hit in the forehead with a shovel. My thoughts were muffled, my emotions nearly numb. It was impossible to concentrate on the task at hand: we had to remove what remained of our friends.

We told ourselves that the crevasses on the glacier had grown too wide in the recent warm weather for us to safely evacuate the bodies. The truth was that we were so emotionally shattered we did not have the heart to do the job by ourselves. Lowering the bodies of McAndrews and Kevin into a crevasse, our team descended the glacier, packed up at base camp, and headed down through the forest. We had to get to the truck, return to Calafate, and find a helicopter. We were an expedition with a mission, much like before. Minus two.

My thoughts were random and unfocused: I guess I can have the harmonica and that new Kelty. I won't have to share what's left of our condensed milk. . . . How can I think things like this?

McAndrews, my best buddy, was dead. So was Kevin.

The one thing I didn't think about was whether they had made it to the summit. It was the furthest thing from my mind and just didn't matter anymore.

Doña Rosa knew the governor; he would personally talk to President Juan Perón, she promised. The president would send a helicopter from Buenos Aires, and once the bodies were "rescued," he would send his private plane to carry them back to the capital.

Around the governor at his heavy oak table sat the battalion of rescuers and newspeople. The only foreigner, I alone did not understand the proceedings. Yet I was responsible for all that had transpired. Since I was to blame for the entire operation, I felt like I should say something. I thumbed through my handy pocket dictionary and looked up the words for "risk" and "gratitude." I tried to thank everyone assembled for spending their money and their time, for making our problem their own, for being such good people. We stood and patted each other on the back. Two men introduced themselves as the pilots who had hauled McAndrews's body from the crevasse. Around their necks they wore silver climbing nuts on familiar, Day-Glow pink nylon. On each one was printed "Welcome to the Freaker's Ball."

After returning to the States, a mutual friend told me that our team had been "in over our heads," that we had foolishly "gotten off route and should have turned back."

Perhaps. But the pain of that thought is too great to bear. The truth is, it's too late now for second-guessing. Of course, I am deeply sorry for the terrible loss that befell Steve's and Kevin's family and friends. Still, I do not think my departed friends would want me to spend my days in weepy regret. If, in the future, I perish in the midst of attempting some daredeviltry, I don't want any friend of mine to do anything but celebrate my passion for living.

In the twenty-five years since his death there are few days I have not thought of Cowboy Steve McAndrews. The only antidote I know for suffering is to focus on the lessons learned, the gift found within the tragedy. I have tried to live more like McAndrews because he is not around to do it for me. I try to remember to dance more often, to try on new attitudes, and to consistently demand more from myself than I used to. A near-death experience has shown me how near to life I wish to remain.

CHAPTER 4

Scale Your Inner Mountaintop

On September 29, 1988, Stacy Allison became the first American woman to stand atop Mount Everest. Sudden celebrity followed: she appeared on *Late Night with David Letterman* and *Good Morning America* and was profiled in such magazines as *Life*, *Time*, *Esquire*, and *Glamour*.

Stacy is slight, almost waiflike, and her petite size makes her accomplishments even more impressive. It is Stacy's spirit that is extra-large. For someone who has spent so much of her life above the clouds, she is extremely down to earth and laughs easily at herself. Her story traces the evolution of a determined adventurer of the spirit.

In 1987, after more than twenty years of leading climbing expeditions around the world—including Pakistan and Russia—Stacy became a member of the North Face American Everest Expedition. Her team spent five days in a snow cave at 23,500 feet, sitting out the worst storm the mountain had seen in forty years. After emerging from their cave and ascending to 25,500 feet, the team found their hefty metal snow pickets blown 150 feet from the route. "The pickets were twisted like licorice whips," remembers Stacy. "It was the most amazing demonstration of power I've ever seen. My respect for the mountain soared. After three days at 25,500 feet and a wind that would not stop blowing, we got off the mountain."

Stacy Allison swore to return. A year later, she did.

"It was summit day on Everest," she recalls. "We drew straws to see who was going to the summit because we had only one oxygen bottle. I won, but my moment of joy was followed by the realization: I am going to the summit without my friends."

Later that day, when Stacy Allison realized a lifelong dream of reaching the 29,028-foot summit, something was missing. "I was on top of the world but I was alone. This wasn't how I wanted it to happen. I wanted to hug someone, to make the dream explode into life by seeing it reflected in someone else's eyes."

Stacy went on to become team leader of a successful expedition to K2 in Pakistan, the earth's second-highest peak and perhaps the toughest mountaineering challenge known to humankind. "Everest is a mountain I describe as 'feminine.' She will let you play on her. She may push you away, but she is always welcoming, letting you return to her again," muses Stacy. "K2, however—all jagged, steep rock and horrific weather—has no feminine aspects. None at all." It was on this climb that teammate Dan Culver fell to his death. Stacy survived.

One minute he was there and the next he wasn't. But it is the strangest thing. You cannot grieve on a mountain. You have to compartmentalize immediately. You can't even allow any dark emotions to enter your thoughts. It is still a survival situation. The day after Dan fell, we woke up to a whiteout blizzard. It was all we could do to get off the mountain alive. The wind was blowing so hard at one point that I unclipped from one rope in order to crawl ten feet to another. All I could do was dig in my ice ax, crampons, and front points, and wait for ten minutes that felt more like an eternity. Wait to be blown completely off the mountain.

Not long ago, the focus of her adventurous life began to shift. This time the arena was not mountaineering but motherhood. Stacy became a working mom, splitting her efforts between marriage, running a couple of businesses, and raising two kids.

"I had waited until I was thirty-seven years old before I had my first child. I had a career; I had a life before children. For thirty-six years I did exactly what I wanted to do and my life was centered on me. I was the universe. Now it is no longer about me. It is about my kids, about allowing them to become healthy, competent, confident human beings."

Though her life is admittedly different, Stacy's enthusiasm is as enormous as ever because, she claims, so is the payoff. Unlike her solitary experience atop Everest, these days her ecstatic moments are shared with her family. No longer does it take a tempest threatening to suck her into space to remind her how good it is to be alive. "Isn't being an adventurer about not getting stuck in one place, but taking on different roles in different situations? What remains the same, no matter the context, is the importance of integrity, treating people fairly. And doing the best I can do."

Lessons Learned by Dying

Too often the education that we require to reexamine our goals comes at a hefty price. These days, anyone with $75,000 can afford tuition for the Mount Everest School of hardship. Unfortunately the price tag is no guarantee of surviving the course. May 10, 1996, marked the worst one-day loss of life in the history of the mountain. Among the confirmed dead was forty-nine-year-old Dallas pathologist Beck Weathers, who had paid his money to take a chance on summiting the world's highest peak. Instead he lay in a hypothermic coma at 22,000 feet, where he had twice been left for dead by other climbers. His wife and family had already been advised of his death when he miraculously awoke and found the strength to rise from beneath a thick layer of snow and ice and stagger into camp. Sixteen hours of exposure to extreme cold and storm conditions would eventually cost him his nose, his right hand, and the fingers of his left hand.

Today Weathers tours the country on the speaker circuit, a survivor of Everest who gives audiences the lessons learned from his ordeal. Chief among those lessons is that what matters most in life is not high adventure in faraway places but the love and care of family and friends at home base. Weathers paid a hefty price for these lessons, but not all Everest climbers are that fortunate. To date, although nearly 800 people have reached the 29,028-foot summit, 160 have died trying.

Adapt Your Itinerary

In any quest for a greater perspective, some detours from the original itinerary are to be expected. Success depends on our willingness to alter our compass bearing and adopt new route plans whenever we discover that our old map no longer accurately describes the territory. Arriving at a precipice, we must admit that the only step forward is one in an entirely new direction.

For some of us the travel plan of choice includes a trip to a locale where the ice drops away 5,000 feet behind our boot heels. We require the periodic dose of danger, the occasional lambada with Lady Luck. For others, personal growth does not require a constant dose of discomfort and repetitive exposure to the wind, the cold, and cranky customs officials. For the adrenaline-addicted I am the bearer of bad news: *Danger may be adventure's song, but adventure is not necessarily danger.* Peak experiences are wherever we decide to find them. Even in our own backyards. Of course, closer to home we may actually have to work a little harder at it.

Taste the Unforgettable Taste

Regardless of outcome or locale, aiming high lands us in unique company. During the long months McAndrews and I spent at Estancia Cristina, exploring our surroundings and plotting our escape, we learned that among the handful of fellow visitors who had dropped in to visit Bert Masters's family over the years was the legendary Antoine de Saint-Exupéry, author of *The Little Prince* and pioneer aviator whose entire life was a paean to the joys of daring.

Lost in the Sahara after a plane crash, dizzy and near death, Saint-Exupéry wrote:

> I have nothing to complain of. For three days I have tramped the desert, have known the pangs of thirst, have followed false scents in the sand, have pinned my faith on the dew. I have struggled to rejoin my kind, whose very existence on earth I had forgotten. These are the cares of men alive in every fiber, and I cannot help thinking them more important than the fretful choosing of a nightclub in which to spend the evening. Compare the one life with the other, and all things considered this is luxury. I have no regrets. I have gambled and lost. It was all in a day's work. At least I have had the unforgettable taste of the sea on my lips.

In 1944, on a reconnaissance mission over the Mediterranean during World War II, Saint-Exupéry disappeared.

To have had the "unforgettable taste of the sea" on our lips; to have sunsets over canyons indelibly etched in our minds; to have watched our children being born and our loved ones dying; to have caught a glimpse of our lives opening in slow motion like flowers unfolding their petals toward the sun; to have seen our fortunes made and lost is to be alive. When we become aware how numbered our days are, it becomes supremely important that we fill that finite number with something beyond the mundane. This is the gift that awareness of our mortality offers us. It impels us to go for the gusto, to insist on an existence of increasing magnitude. An awareness of death ups the ante on life.

Stay on the Cutting Edge

"There is an exciting phase in any career, and then people tend to graduate from it. I made a decision to stay at it," says Dr. Bob Ballard, undersea explorer, discoverer of the *Titanic*, and adventure entrepreneur extraordinaire. "I refused advancing in my military career beyond the position of commander because if you are a captain you're not welcome aboard nuclear submarines. And I enjoy going aboard nuclear submarines. Going on expeditions was the most exciting part of my work, so I made a very calculated career decision. I structured my life so I could stay where the excitement, the energy, and the cutting edge are."

If anyone is qualified to talk about a life spent on the cutting edge it is Bob Ballard. He has achieved considerable fame and fortune by aiming not high but deep. It was after watching Ballard's 1987 *National Geographic* documentary that James Cameron got the idea to make a movie about the *Titanic*. In addition to the *Titanic*, Ballard has discovered ancient Roman shipwrecks in the Tyrrhenian Sea, the legendary German battleship *Bismarck*, and life forms previously unknown to science on the edge of hydrothermal vents near the Galápagos Islands. Recently, he located the USS *Yorktown*, the aircraft carrier lost in the Battle of Midway and the deepest shipwreck ever found.

Having completed his 110th underwater expedition and seen more of the ocean floor than any other human being, Ballard is undoubtedly one of the world's great modern explorers.

"To be an explorer is to have a dream," says Ballard. "Your dream gives your life direction and helps you navigate day-to-day decisions. Let your dream inform your life: look at opportunities through the dream's filter and ask yourself whether any given situation will move you closer to fulfilling it."

In 1985, on the way back from the Azores to his home base in Wood's Hole, Massachusetts, Bob Ballard realized one of his long-held dreams. His team was about 800 miles from home when their "unofficial search" hit the jackpot: from two and a half miles down, never-before-seen images of the sunken *Titanic* began to stream in, supplied by the *Argo*, Ballard's submersible photographic robot.

"Suddenly there it was," he says. "A disaster put to rest over seventy years ago came roaring back into the present like a freight train. The ship was cut completely in half. You could see a cross section of a six-story building, the grand ballroom under the forward skylight, and then the grand staircase taking you down to the first-class accommodations."

But of all the sights that greeted Ballard that amazing day, one nearly knocked him to the floor: the empty lifeboat davits without boats. "To me that was the symbolism of the *Titanic*— the empty lifeboat davits. Exactly what the people who died saw as they desperately searched for a lifeboat. To finally emerge from the second or third class to the boat deck and find all the lifeboats gone. Gone! And there it was in the picture. We came over the top with that *Argo*, saw the picture, and—slam—it was like a fist to my stomach."

Ballard describes the *Titanic* as a tomb. "It is," he says, "the first pyramid of the sea." Obsessed by the enormous amount of human history still buried beneath the ocean's surface, he has plans for further explorations, especially in the Mediterranean, where literally hundreds of ancient wrecks await discovery. Obviously, Bob Ballard believes in setting sky-high (or in his case, ocean-deep) standards for personal performance. "I've got thousands of projects in different stages," he tells me. "I'm off to the Amazon for three weeks to do our Jason Project, then to the Sinai to look at a Phoenician ship."

Bob has a few other irons in the fire: there is an upcoming expedition to the Black Sea, lots of lecturing and book writing, three TV specials in production, a CD-ROM, plus a house, a new research center, and a new exhibition hall all under construction. "It's just not that hard," he explains with a smile. "Once you learn how to do it."

Choose the Biggest Challenges

According to Bob Ballard, mastering the art of peak performance begins with setting "extraordinarily elevated goals." The advantages of aiming high, he says, are threefold:

> First, if you climb a mountain that's 1,000 feet tall and you fall 600 feet, you're toast. Whereas if you climb a mountain that is 30,000 feet and fall off it, you are toast anyway. The point is, why not go for it because the risks are comparable. Second, the higher the mountain, the fewer the folks who are trying. There is less competition with a bigger challenge so you actually have a higher probability of success. Third, the bigger the challenge, the longer it takes and the fewer the number of smaller challenges you need to take on along the way. If I choose a project that is going to take ten years, I don't have to think of another one for ten more years. That aspect of the challenge keeps you in the game for a long time.

Pick a Lofty Goal

Having a lofty objective serves as a handy reference point when facing the challenges of daily life. "If you don't have a goal, there is no purpose to your life, you are just sailing around," says Ballard.

> Even after you have found a star on the horizon, you realize there is no direct path. There are always options. Each day you weigh opportunities; you can pick A, B, C, or D. None of these may be pointing at your goal, but you pick the one that's closest to it. You go down that path until it's necessary to tack back the other way. That's because if you continue on the first path, eventually you are going to be moving away from your goal. Each tack provides you with a new perspective, a new reality. The important thing is to be alert, stay flexible, and keep on sailing.
>
> You have that marker buoy out there and you are tacking on it. It is helping you make decisions. And what's amazing is that you get there! The great realization is that you can get there. And that reinforces you to say, "Hell, anything is possible!"

Prepare to Fail

Although conventional wisdom admonishes us to "visualize success," Bob Ballard insists on the opposite: prepare to fail. Humans learn best by trial and error, and less effectively by trial and success. Our successes naturally end in self-congratulation and celebration, but our failures move us into even more useful terrain. Failure tends to encourage introspection and a willingness to start afresh. Likewise, setbacks help us cast off old assumptions and come up with new possibilities.

"Success is not a measure of avoiding failure," says Ballard.

Success is processing failure. You must pass through failure to get to success. It is not a thing you avoid. A lot of people have been taught to avoid failure, but I don't think they can succeed unless they pass through it. I've seen a lot of people who started out with everything working to their advantage, except when they faced failure for the first time they couldn't process it. They weren't conditioned to fail.

Building an acceptance—even an expectation—of failure into our personal and professional lives allows us to thrive, even in moments of extreme disappointment. At the organizational level, a company whose culture is informed by the way of adventure recognizes innovation and risk taking as essential for success. In this climate, paradigm busting and out-of-the-box thinking are considered worthy of praise.

Great leaps forward in our lives are inevitably anticipated by a few sorry stumbles; imaginative experimentation and looking foolish may go hand in hand. Not surprisingly, the most successful and forward-thinking organizations with which I have worked all have a similar operating principle: Reward the fool who fails rather than the stalwart who has learned to play it safe. Greatness belongs to those who are unafraid to fail, mediocrity to those who insist on always succeeding.

Aim Higher Than Everest

I once heard Willi Unsoeld, one of the great philosopher-climbers of our time, speak about the expedition that placed him among the first Americans atop the highest summit on the planet, and about the depression that plagued him afterward: "You've climbed the biggest mountain in the world. What's left?

Disappointment. You realize you have accomplished your dream. It is literally all downhill from there." He paused and looked over the crowd. "You've got to set your sights on something higher than Everest."

A wise climber never forgets that the mountain is only a metaphor. The landscape of ice field and spire is a canvas for the highest form of performance art. Mountaineering is a vertical dance, poetry in motion. So why aim high? Because up there is where the view is. The long ridge looms before us, steeper than anything we have yet tackled. From within, we summon strengths we did not know we possessed, stamina of both body and will. Our spirit grows larger as the task before us magnifies. As we rise to the challenge, we come to find that peak experiences are ours whenever we labor in the direction of our dreams, setting goals that exceed our easy grasp. The reward for aiming high is less the fleeting moment of victory than the ongoing discovery of our capacity for greatness.

Remember That Stranger Things Have Happened

I recall a solo climb in Patagonia where I was attempting to reach a previously unattained, snowy summit on the edge of the ice cap. There was a remote but shimmering possibility of a mixed ascent route along the north ridge; a single band of unclimbable ice or rock would have been sufficient to halt my hard-earned progress. It was illogical to start at all, but the allure of a "first ascent" drew me upward despite the stacked (and towering) odds against success. Time and time again I found myself facing an impassable obstacle, and in my head I would hear a sober voice suggesting, "Turn back—before it is too late." Then I would hear another, more idealistic voice: "Don't give up! Keep on. There might be a way through. Stranger things have happened." And then I would spy a snowbridge, a foothold, a difficult but doable way past the obstacle that didn't seem to have been there a moment before. Soon, *stranger things have happened* became a mantra leading me steadily upward, miraculously undoing every seemingly terminal obstacle. By midafternoon I found myself alone on a major Patagonian summit. It was the high point of a lifetime, a point that I had reckoned to be impossible only hours before.

Renew the View

We can only become as large as our mission. A goal set at a comfortable height allows us to be mildly successful. Only a goal that forces us to stretch can make us wildly successful. "Life shrinks or expands in proportion to one's courage," wrote the author Anaïs Nin. A great undertaking inspires us to acts of true imagination and daring. If our days take us nowhere, it is not because we have aimed too high but because we have set our sights too low.

We cannot see the summit from the parking lot; the view enlarges as we ascend. In fact, the view never has been as good as it is right now. And right now. And again, right now. Especially in times of change, success is the result of a practiced ability to let go of all preconceptions in the face of new information. The alternative? A life of "false summits."

Stay True to Your Path

Feeling passionate about life is a natural by-product of aiming high. Maintaining that passion becomes the challenge. First we must determine for ourselves which goals are appropriate and in what direction our adventure lies; then we must commit to steering in that direction—even in the face of societal pressure to take a more conventional life or career path.

Wisdom accrues over time. I did not understand this back at FitzRoy, when our happy and glorious expedition turned to mud. Everything I thought I knew suddenly seemed wrong; nothing made sense. For a year after the accident I could not see straight, could not channel my thoughts. I laughed and cried at the wrong times. Moments of exhilaration alternated with depression. All I knew was that I hurt and I hurt badly. I had fallen into what Joseph Campbell labeled the "Pit of Despair" on the Hero's Journey. I had to find a way to climb out. At least, I reckoned, climbing was something I knew how to do.

Make Your Own Adventures

1. GET UNREAL

Any adventure worth the name is inspired by an outlandish goal. Adventuring is the process of connecting all the dots between an unrealistic objective and a successful outcome. If you were king of the world, if you did run the zoo . . . what would your life be like? Here's how to get started on bringing the unlikely to life:

> *Make a "dream list" of your ideal job, your perfect home or travel environment, your happiest ideal for a relationship. Be creative, imaginative, even unrealistic. Now list the likely action steps to your wild goals. Then, without expectation of success, start connecting the dots.*

What would you really like to do? Host your own TV show? Earn the job of your boss, or even a better one? Build new facilities at your child's public school? Heal a chronic, painful relationship with a family member? Save an old-growth forest? Stamp out greed and injustice? Too often our efforts meet with a lack of success because we have not set the bar high enough to engage the full power of our adventurous spirit. Instead our life enters a limbo in the truest sense of the word: we get used to knocking the bar down a peg to see how low we can go.

As Henry David Thoreau wrote about living the life of his dreams at Walden Pond: "I learned this, at least, by my experiment: that if one advances confidently in the direction of his dreams, and endeavors to live the life which he has imagined, he will meet with a success unexpected in common hours. . . . If you have built castles in the air, your work need not be lost; that is where they should be. Now put foundations under them."

When all looks lost and only illogic suggests that "keeping the faith" is worth the effort, carry on. You just might succeed—or at any rate end up in a far different place from where you started toward your unlikely goal. Remember: stranger things have happened. The key is to maximize your imagination, your adaptability, and your capacity to learn from failure.

2. JUST SAY YES

Volunteering for a task or activity we are not good at—or have habitually resisted—is a balm for rigid and inflated egos. There is no laughter more liberating than our own when it's aimed at ourselves.

> *Act out of character. Try one thing at which you are wholly inexperienced, historically no good, or stubbornly resistant.*

Be it a graceless attempt at juggling, waterskiing, or singing opera, what do you have to lose by trying except your pride? Next time someone invites you to a game of racquetball, a tango lesson, or a cooking class, just say yes and see what happens. The key is to expect failure, but be willing to experience the delight of a novel and invigorating experience.

In the final scene of the film *Never Cry Wolf*, an old Eskimo shaman who has proven his mastery of both physical and spiritual realms sits beside the city-boy protagonist who is painstakingly learning the ways of wild nature. Amused, the wizened shaman looks on while the city fellow attempts to juggle a handful of oranges. The master decides to give it a try. The viewer is set up to assume that the shaman will be a natural, his beginner's mind and natural grace allowing him to handily master this simple entertainment on the first attempt. He flings the oranges into the air and the fruit flies in all directions, none of it returning remotely close to his flailing hands. A wide smile of delight spreads across the old man's face, as if he has just experienced the best and truest outcome of his playful experiment.

The lesson of this heartwarming scene is that failure is not only a better teacher than success, it can even be more fun—if we let it. Indeed, if laughter is the best therapy, the willingness to laugh at ourselves is the sign of true mental health.

3. APPRECIATE ADVERSITY

The Dalai Lama says, "Easy times are the enemy, they put us to sleep. Adversity is our greatest friend, it wakes us up. Similarly, our dearest friend is not as good a teacher as our worst enemy." Here's an opportunity to give positive acknowledgment to whatever is in your way.

> *Take some time to make notes on your toughest current obstacle, your greatest personal weakness, or your meanest adversary. Then jot down the corresponding strength or potential that you need to develop to overcome the challenges presented by each obstacle you've listed. Finally, write down "thank you's" for all the challenges that are providing you with reasons and directions for growth.*

Just as the dentist's drill alerts us to sensitive areas, so do our responses of impatience, anger, or hostility alert us to the cavities in our soul. Whether it be a mountain, a performance standard, a sales quota, or a marathon, every kind of challenge pits us against our chief internal adversary—ourselves.

Mahatma Gandhi once reflected that he faced three great adversaries in life. The first was the government of Great Britain, which he found the easiest to persuade and overcome. The second, more difficult challenge was his own people, the people of India. And his third great opponent—the one that he found the most difficult to change—was himself.

Gandhi achieved the liberation of an entire nation in part because he approached his task from a deep spiritual perspective. That's where the second part of this exercise comes in—the application of spiritual values like forgiveness, acceptance, and appreciation. As the Vajrayana school of Tibetan Buddhism reminds us, the higher the summit, the steeper the climb, and the whiter the water, the greater the potential for growth that is presented to us. The more we can positively appreciate our opposition, the greater the strength we nurture within ourselves. With enough practice of this exercise, you will discover that the kind of challenges that used to send you reeling have become the source of a deep and productive way of life.

Give It All You've Got

Full effort is full victory.

—Mahatma Gandhi

NEVADA WIER

Intiyampu, Raft of the Sun,
Lake Titicaca, Bolivia

CHAPTER 5

Sailing in the Wake of the Sun Gods

"**A**dventure? I've got a great one for you," confided my friend, the professional outdoor photographer Nevada Wier, over a cold Bohemia and a plate of cheese enchiladas at our local Mexican eatery on a sunny day in June 1978. In conspiratorial whispers Nevada spoke of a lake on the border of Bolivia and Peru where the Aymara Indians, descendants of a mysterious, pre-Inca civilization called Tiahuanaco, still live in near-total isolation. She was reading a book that told of hidden monasteries where mystic monks had achieved such high levels of consciousness that levitation was a routine feature of daily meditation.

Nevada excitedly told me about one of the Inca legends. Inti, the great sun god, didn't like the idea of humans living like animals so he decided to send his son and daughter, Manco Capac and Mama Ocllo, to teach them how to live properly. They arrived at a spot called the Island of the Sun and decided to build a boat from the reeds. Then they sailed the entire lake teaching people how to weave, spin, and farm. When they had done all that, they climbed over the Andes and started the Inca Empire.

"No one has ever repeated that experience," Nevada con-
cluded with a wink. I just shrugged in reply, not catching her
drift. If Indiana Jones and Anaïs Nin had ever gotten together,
their offspring would have been Nevada Wier. She continued
impatiently: "Jeff, what if we went to Bolivia, built a boat from
reeds, and became the first people in modern times to circum-
navigate the world's highest lake in a traditional boat? What if we
replicated the voyage of the ancient sun gods?"

I knew enough geography to realize that Nevada was talking
about Lake Titicaca, the frigid inland sea of the Andes—at
12,500 feet, the world's highest navigable waterway. But to sail it
in a reed boat, following in the wake of ancient gods? It sounded
ridiculous, far-fetched, undoubtedly dangerous.

"Sure," I said. "Why not?"

When you begin doing things that no one has ever done, it
doesn't take too long to discover why no one has gone before
you. There is a reason there are no reed boats left on Lake Titicaca. They are all under Lake Titicaca. Because reed boats don't
float—at least not for long.

But the locale of Nevada's proposed "sun gods tour" was challenging in other ways as well. If there is a territory on the planet
where Cheshire cats and talking caterpillars would feel at home,
the otherworldly landscape of the Andean altiplano around Lake
Titicaca is it. You see, Bolivia is where the planet holds its Mad
Hatter tea parties.

In the squalor and confusion outside the airports you first
notice the natives. The deeply sculpted, impassive faces of the
men stare at you from beneath crazy cone-shaped hats, like
turnips set upside down. The women are bulky figures in colorful fringed shawls shuffling along in black rubber pumps and
knee-length polleras—party dresses of pink, blue and yellow—
that are parodies of those worn by the Spanish colonial women
of the nineteenth century. Above gray or jet black hair pulled

tightly into braids, the women also sport bowler hats set at a rakish tilt. These are the Aymara, the original inhabitants of the region, whose world is filled with mischievous spirits. For them the paramount virtue is cunning, not honesty.

Built on the side of an enormous crater, La Paz, the world's highest capital, reminds me of an enormous sports arena. Over a million people crowd the bleachers in a site chosen originally by a handful of Spanish conquistadores to escape the maddening winds of the high plain. Wealthy families claiming a pure European lineage have the prime infield seats down below in the affluent communities of Calacoto and Obrajes, whereas the indigenous campesinos content themselves with the cheaper seats in the stands above. At night the stadium comes to life with light.

This is Bolivia, cheapest ticket on this earth for a journey to another world. Bolivia has remained the poorest, highest, and most remote republic in South America. Sixty percent of its foreign exchange comes from cocaine, three-quarters of its population can't read or write, and after losing every war it has ever entered, the government still talks about attacking Chile to win back a beach town or two.

Six weeks after cooking up our absurd plan, Nevada and I were staggering, too—running from office to office in the capital at 11,000 feet, attempting to obtain all the requisite papers from the proper bureaucrats. If we thought the locals were a bit disreputable, they certainly thought no better of us. The Peruvian consulate informed us our trip would bring us across the border into their territory, where there was no immigration post; thus our plan was illegal and we would have to give it up. The Bolivian navy was even tougher. We hadn't expected to deal with the navy in a landlocked country, but this was Bolivia.

Finally we resorted to a tried-and-true American strategy: we announced our intentions to the local press and were interviewed on television and by the newspapers. Soon we were national celebrities just for coming up with such an audacious plan. The navy and other obstreperous government agencies relented and decided to let two foolhardy gringos risk their lives on Lake Titicaca after all. The Peruvians were still not impressed, but we decided that if we made it that far we'd resort to the oldest trick in the book, common to ten-year-olds and expedition professionals: it is always easier to say you're sorry afterward than to get permission beforehand. One problem remained: we had to get a reed boat somehow. And it had to float, at least for a while.

Of the boat builders we met by the lakeshore, only Samuel Choque never told us that we were completely nuts. You could see through the holes in Choque's blue cardigan, but his gray eyes were opaque and inscrutable. Choque was an Aymara born and raised along the lakeshore, a crafty survivor who knew more of the lake's secrets than any living soul. He found for us some of the same craftsmen who had made the *Ra II* for Thor Heyerdahl, and over several weeks he supervised the making of the largest reed boat ever to sail upon Titicaca.

I was nervous about trusting Choque at first, but Nevada convinced me that we had no choice. After all, Choque was on a first-name basis with the *achachilas*, or grandfather spirits of the lake, to whom the locals regularly offer tobacco, coca leaf, candy, and strong drink. The sight of these economically deprived people throwing their prized indulgences into the water for the benefit of the gods is not soon forgotten by possessive *norteamericanos*. But then, we didn't grow up on the shores of the legendary Titicaca.

At the center of the Aymara cosmos is the sacred lake, surrounded by summits of 20,000 feet sending down fierce winds that stir up whirlpools and generate huge waves crashing against rock islands and sheer cliffs. Comprising 3,200 square miles of icy glacial runoff reaching a depth of a thousand feet, Titicaca is more of an inland sea than a lake. Taking Samuel Choque at his word, Nevada and I would sail his creation into the realm of the *achachilas* where, before us, only a son and daughter of the sun god had dared to tread.

Every journalist in the country was there to watch us hoist anchor. There were officials from the UN, the U.S. Embassy, several tourist groups, and a gang of rough-cut travel folk from the Residencial Illimani hotel—a motley assortment of backpackers hailing from New Zealand to Belgium who, during the endless weeks of preparation, had become our late-night party buddies and emotional support team. Like any wanderers deserving of the name, they enthusiastically took advantage of the free food and champagne provided by a La Paz–based insurance company that had decided to "sponsor" us.

The craft was spectacularly beautiful. The *Inti Yampu*—Raft of the Sun—was twenty-five feet of golden reeds, its long upturned bow festooned with red cantuti flowers and yellow daisies. The wife of the insurance company's president tried to break a bottle of cheap champagne on the grassy bow, but it bounced instead. Speeches were made. Exceedingly large amounts of beer and candy were offered to the *achachilas*; it looked like the natives thought we could use all the divine help we could get. With the drinks left, boisterous toasts were made to what the local press hailed as "one of the greatest sailing adventures of our time."

At dusk, we slipped away toward the Strait of Tiquina. Our departure was clumsy, but at least no one was there to watch. Only Choque remained on the dock, waving silently.

We were silent, too, because we were exceedingly anxious. Earlier that day Nevada had admitted that she had never really sailed before. I found this bit of news quite alarming. I had been counting on her skills—because not only had I never sailed, I could barely even swim.

On the first night out, we found ourselves stuck in the middle of the strait. Dripping wet, we huddled together beneath the inadequate refuge of our one-room straw house amidships while rain poured down upon us by the bucketful. Since the balsa is an ancient vessel, it has no keel and, therefore, cannot tack. It sails with the wind or not at all. Although we were hardly seasoned navigators, Nevada and I determined that the wind was definitely not in our favor. We dropped anchor. Our boat filled like a bathtub, bounced like a rubber ducky.

By day three we had visited and left the Bolivian navy dock at Tiquina. We entered the big waters of Titicaca. A brisk wind allowed us to plow into a safe harbor at a cove populated with fishing boats and planted in eucalyptus. Then for nearly a week, gales kept us pinned to the shore, waiting in our tent.

With a lot of spare time on my hands, I walked the rocky shoreline not knowing whether to pray for a good wind or a sudden end to our expedition. It had begun to dawn on me that of all my undertakings so far, this was the most bizarre. The magnitude of our adventure was enormous: the lake seemed as endless as an ocean, and its typical weather would make Cape Horn look like a vacation in the Bahamas. The constant rocking of the boat in the waves made me seasick.

After our festive send-off, the natives' reception was almost as chilly as the waters of the lake. Everyone we met spoke to us in Aymara or not at all. When they dared to approach us, they inevitably shook their pointy-hatted heads. Some laughed, riotously. A couple of especially theatrical fishermen mimed our demise, banging their heads with rocks and falling, melodramatically, to the ground.

After several days, we could take no more. Ignoring seasoned advice and our own intuition, we headed out into a changing wind and were carried right back to our starting point at Tiquina. Daunted but undefeated, we took a few days' break and ventured forth once more.

Slowly we gained familiarity with our rigging and learned how to find friendly patches of reeds where we could drop our two anchors and catch some sleep. One night near Thajocachi, a storm caused us to slip anchor, forcing our boat onto the gravelly beach. Rocks ate big mouthfuls of reeds from the side and ripped apart our ropes. Nevada and I somehow managed to pull the *Inti Yampu* back into the waves; another few minutes and she would have been little more than a few tons of grass clippings. The next day, local schoolkids helped us with repairs when the two of us, numb and shaking, could no longer stand the 50-degree waters.

A Gift to the Spirits

Along a deserted coast north of Kakachi, we were dined by a barrel-chested Aymara fisherman named Bonafacio Nina Chacón and his daughter Maxima in their crumbly mud home. A calendar from the previous year with a photograph of a chubby, poncho-weaving *cholita*—a Bolivian countrywoman of Indian descent—was all that adorned the walls. The kitchen, dining room, and bedroom were the same one room. The fare was a small potful of potatoes. Ceremoniously our host scooped up much of the contents of the pot and with a guttural "Cchua achachilas!" tossed them onto the earth outside the house.

I was stunned. "Why did you throw out that food?" I asked.

Our host smiled paternally as he doled out the remainder of the boiled potatoes. "You probably think that those potatoes are wasted. It is not so. They are a gift to the grandfather spirits, the *achachilas*, the spirit of the lake, the spirit of this place." He gestured in a circle around our humble surroundings and added, "You see, everything is alive. Everything has a personality. Westerners think the world is a machine to be controlled. The Aymara know it is pure spirit and can never be controlled or even understood. *There is one simple rule: you must give more than you can afford. And be grateful for whatever you receive. Always.*"

Emerging from a night of camaraderie, returning to our boat, we found our line had been cut. Only a miracle had kept the *Inti Yampu* and everything we owned from blowing into the middle of the lake and disappearing beneath the waves forever.

"The *achachilas*," murmured Bonafacio.

"Saved the boat, or cut the rope?" we wondered.

"Quién sabe?" he responded. Who knows?

One month passed. Then two. Nevada and I slowly became passable reed-boat sailors, accumulating a lifetime's worth of extraordinary sights and experiences along the way. Along the empty mudflats of the Ramis Peninsula, what we thought to be a distant community of pink houses took to the air a few dozen feet in front of us: a flock of wild flamingos. Near Chaguaya, a fleet of Aymaras in their own small boats came to greet us. When the winds turned against us, they threw us ropes and, bending to their oars, pulled us for miles along the coast. We were entranced by a sense of magic and impressed by the humility of people giving far more than they could afford to us—and to the *achachilas*.

In Pusi we became godparents to a young Quechua girl and learned a crucial lesson about teamwork. Eight weeks into a trip we had hoped would entail only a few, Nevada and I were suffering a distinct loss of morale. Once the best of travel companions, we had virtually ceased talking to each other. Our expeditionary efficiency had plummeted as a result. We hoped that a little onshore leave would raise our flagging spirits. Unfortunately, our host Hipolito couldn't provide much in the way of a fiesta.

Clustered around a smoky fire fueled by an acrid cocktail of sheep and cow dung, we fortified our spirits with a bottle of high-octane corn distillate that represented the equivalent of the family's monthly earnings. We were the first outsiders to have ever come ashore in this ancient world. Having performed the ritual first haircut on Hipolito's tiny daughter Vincentina and offered our presents of oranges, bananas, and peanuts, Nevada and I had made a fast new friend. Accordingly, he entrusted us with a confession.

Apologizing for the meagerness of the celebration, Hipolito admitted that he was worried about the survival of his family. His cows had died and his lambs would not last much longer on their diet of dried barley stalks, the only feed he could provide. Neighbors had planted their fields so densely that they had left no outlet to the lake where Hipolito could graze his animals on the only feed the environment provided, the water plants called chanko that clogged the shore. He had asked his neighbors to leave some small access to the lake. They had responded that they required every available square foot and furrow along the lakeshore to keep their families alive.

A motorized pump was the obvious solution, we suggested. It could pull fresh water from the lake and irrigate the countless acres of arable land that now lay dry and fallow just a few hundred feet away from the water's edge. After an initial investment it would solve everyone's problem, increasing the wealth of every family a hundredfold.

Our host shook his head dismissively. With tears in his tired eyes he said, "La gente estan trabajando en contra. No saben trabajar juntas." People are working against each other. They don't know how to work together.

Back on our boat that night, Nevada and I found our boat surrounded by chanko, unable to move. Using my oar as a pole I pulled in one direction, Nevada pulled in the other. We wobbled back and forth, going nowhere. Finally free, Nevada rowed in one direction. I rowed in the other. We were turning in circles, each of us too stubborn to give in. The setting sun found us stopped dead in the water, hurling complaints at each other, airing out weeks of petty resentments and imagined injustices.

Finally Nevada pointed out that just like Hipolito's community, we were working not with but against each other. But in our case the truth was painfully obvious: we were literally in the same boat. We had to laugh. There could be no claim to the high ground on a flat lake. I needed to help Nevada be all she could be, to assist her in every way possible in order to attain my goal, a successful circumnavigation of Titicaca. Nevada, in turn, needed me to be confident, content, and fully functional for the same end. So we agreed to work together again.

What we had hoped would be the final day of our trip nearly became the final day of our life. Three months had come and gone; by this time our boat was disintegrating into a floating heap of compost, literally alive with green mold and white larvae. Fortunately for us human stowaways, the Strait of Tiquina was in view and a morning wind blew favorably from the north. "Today's the day!" we laughed. But not for long.

Out of the east came a gale, turning the swells into troughs, filling our sail till it threatened to pull the mast, cables and all, from the boat. Though sodden and soggy, the *Inti Yampu* raced like an outrigger over the waves, moving faster than we had ever moved before. Ahead of us loomed a solid wall of rock.

"Lower the sail!" yelled Nevada, pulling on the rudder with all the strength she possessed.

I did, but it was no use. Our haystack had turned into a hydrofoil, careening out of control, bearing us headlong toward destruction. Beyond pain, beyond exhaustion, we pulled at our oars in a desperate attempt to guide ourselves southward past the heightening row of cliffs.

"Oh my God! *Noooo . . .* ," gasped Nevada. She stared over the side of the boat at the oar that had slipped her grasp, now roller-coasting up and down through the huge swells. "We need that oar!"

This was an understatement; without that oar we were history. Now all we could do was hold on to the bucking balsa for dear life until we were dashed against the rocks. How could it end like this? Had we taken the lake too lightly? Or had the lake gods simply tired of two presumptuous, heathen foreigners? Our adventure epic, often punctuated with slapstick by our amateurish antics as novice sailors, seemed about to end in tragedy. Shaking with cold and exhaustion, we gaped at each other in stunned disbelief. We were going down. . . .

Then, suddenly, an utter stillness fell upon us. The winds had died to nothing, even more quickly than the gale had arisen. Now there was not even a breeze. Our jaws hung open. In more than a hundred days the winds had never simply changed from gusts to gone in a matter of seconds.

Soon the dead calm was followed by a gentle breeze blowing sweetly from the north. It made no sense. Even the swells had diminished to a friendly level, and now they were coming off the rock wall itself, moving us out of harm's way. Amazed and trembling, we hoisted sail. The breeze carried us south until dusk, when we glided right into our old parking place at the navy dock in Tiquina. From the shore we must have looked like old hands, professional sailors. Although not yet safely back at our starting point at Huatajata, we had now successfully circled the lake.

That night, in celebration, Nevada and I shared our remaining food with the sailors who came down to join our cooking fire by the boat. There was peanut butter, strawberry jam, powdered milk, and chocolate.

"Cchua achachilas!" cried a diminutive sailor in a torn uniform, repeating the oath as he threw a handful of precious Hershey bars into the water.

"What are you doing?" I yelled, rushing to stop him before all of our treasures disappeared into the dark lake. "Stop that! I don't care if you eat them, but no more payoffs to these spirits. We've survived already! And we never gave anything to the *achachilas*," I huffed. By now I was convinced that this Aymara tradition wasn't a religion but rather a metaphysical extortion racket.

The sailor smiled and shook his head. "Of course, you are right. By the way, you seem to be missing an oar. How did you get back without it?"

A shiver ran down my spine as Nevada and I exchanged nervous glances. We had to recognize that we had recently been at the mercy of extraordinary forces that pushed us beyond our limits and demanded from us more than we could afford to give—like our oar, among other things. Something or someone had led us to the edge of oblivion, then graciously given us back our lives. Certainly we had much for which to be grateful.

Two days later we arrived at our starting point, Huatajata, where a handful of local Aymara folk lined the dock to greet us. As we clambered off the boat a voice growled from the back of the crowd: "They said you could not have sailed the entire lake. But one look at that poor balsa and I can see that you must have done it." Samuel Choque stepped forward, shook our hands, and said gravely, "Congratulations." He tilted his head toward the listing *Inti Yampu* before smiling warmly and adding, "I am proud of you."

Now we were truly done.

CHAPTER 6

Create a Generous Reality

According to Aymara cosmology, every aspect of the world—every stone, every river, every tree—is alive and gifted with its own personality. Long before the advent of the Western science of ecology, the Aymara knew that everything from earth to sky was not only connected but intimately related. The Aymara universe is one big family, and it's just as cantankerous, quarrelsome, and mixed up as any human clan. Nonetheless, the Aymara live with the faith that generosity of spirit will always be repaid—usually by an unseen source from an unexpected direction.

The Aymara of Bolivia are not the victims of some cosmic extortion racket after all. They view their offerings to the *achachilas* as a way to prime the pump in the cycle of generosity. From the rational, modern point of view, our experience with the lost oar and the mysterious gale was just a strange series of inexplicable accidents. But I had to admit that the Aymara explanation felt more true to my heart and my wave-weary gut: the *achachilas* had decided to teach us a lesson and then let us go.

Practice the Art of Sacrifice

Sacrifice is not a word that puts modern folks at ease. Either we conjure up visions of burning at the stake or we fear that someone will force us to turn down our thermostats and air conditioners. Traditional cultures haven't forgotten the ancient meaning of sacrifice as a way of balancing karmic accounts: sometimes you have to give something up so the gods will give down.

For the adventurer, there are also strictly pragmatic advantages to learning the art of sacrifice. The only way to cover long distances over rough territory is to travel light. You have to jettison the superfluous—and more. Begin by giving up what you don't really need, progressing to some of that which you think you cannot do without. On any serious trek of the body or the spirit, success hinges on the ability to distinguish what is truly and absolutely necessary to persist.

This winnowing process was aptly described by Michelangelo, who was supposedly asked one day how he sculpted masterpieces like *David*, *Moses*, and the *Pietà*. They say that he replied, "I did not sculpt them. All I had to do was to carve away that which was not them."

In psychological terms, the sacrifice asked of us is to surrender the baser aspects of our nature so that our lives can become works of art. Each of us has the potential to live a masterpiece, and for each of us the path to completing that masterpiece is unique. We have to discern which aspects are essential to expressing our inner potential and which aspects—usually our judgments, fears, and addictions—we need to leave behind.

Take Delight in the Process

My journey on Lake Titicaca was my baptism by balsa into a life of renewed faith. Both spiritually and psychologically, I had never been so out of my element as when I ventured forth on that adventure. I learned something about being at the mercy of forces far larger than myself.

It's not that I found some comforting explanation for the tragedy that befell my previous expedition. Instead I realized the futility of attempting to figure it all out. Surviving the voyage of the *Inti Yampu* helped me relinquish the need to understand and rationalize everything that happens. I took in at least a little of the weather-beaten Aymara faith that despite the capriciousness of the gods, there is a basic goodness at work in the universe. When we take delight in the process, we can have faith in the outcome.

Recently, after a talk for the winners of a major life insurance company's performance awards, a woman approached with her husband Bob, a warm and enthusiastic top performer whom I had met earlier in the day. "I get it now!" Bob's wife exclaimed. "I understand why my husband is so happy. I'll never ask him to hold back again. I used to be afraid he would run out of steam. Now I see that it is the giving that keeps him going!"

Whether you're sitting in an office or parasailing across an ice cap, that truth remains the same: it is the giving that keeps us going. That's because we give a great gift to ourselves whenever we are truly there for others.

Contribute to Others' Success

Bill McDermott, a senior vice president in sales and service for the Xerox Corporation, is a living example that giving to others brings its own rewards. His burning drive for success is tempered by a deeply felt concern for the well-being of others.

"I feel that I have something to give. And when I give of myself one hundred percent, I add value to people's lives—both their work lives and their personal lives. If I can touch their spirit, recognizing the commitment it takes to do this job well and the number of hours it takes from a person's life, I feel that I've touched them in a way that's added value to my own life as well."

Bill's track record shows a dynamic achiever who has learned what it takes to be consistently on top. In high school he took over a delicatessen business and managed it so successfully he was able to put himself through college. He started with Xerox twenty-one years ago in New York City, a novice salesman knocking on cold doors for a living. He kept knocking until he was the company's number one salesperson nationwide. He kept this up for three straight years and was rewarded with his first sales team, serving Harlem and the Bronx. Soon his team was first in the country, breaking every record at Xerox. After taking two other teams to the top spot, Bill ran superior sales operations for the New York area, then Puerto Rico, then Chicago. After being promoted to vice president for the central region of the United States, he took over sales and services for the whole country, shattering every growth record in the company.

The secret of his success? Giving. "If you spend enough time figuring out what it is that makes other people successful," he explains, "you spend a lot less time worrying about yourself. You are already successful and happy because you're constantly in a giving mode."

Practice Servant Leadership

This emphasis on giving has rewarded Bill with the two most valuable assets in business today: loyal customers and loyal employees. "When I offer my people promotions in other divisions of the company they usually turn me down," Bill reports.

"They are willing to be positioned less favorably in order to be a part of something unique and somewhat magical. We strive to create a loyalty approach: we're loyal to the client, loyal to our value system, and loyal to excellence."

According to Bill McDermott, loyalty derives from servant leadership (a term coined by business visionary Robert Greenleaf):

When people are down and out, that's when they really need a leader the most—someone who will put an arm around them and say, "I'm here. I'm with you and we're going to get this done. I am personally committed to you." But what they're used to hearing is that they're being talked about in the upstairs office: "Well, he used to be good but he's slipping. He doesn't have the work ethic like he used to. Get rid of him." But I have a natural belief in humans and the human spirit. I believe that people are good and they want to be successful. It's a matter of finding the root of people's difficulties so we can help them be successful.

Take Care of the Whole Person

Servant leadership pays attention to more than performance difficulties from nine to five, McDermott insists:

I work from a perspective that I call the twenty-four-hour person. What that means is recognition of an employee's whole life, not just his or her time at the office. For instance, you have to recognize that a spouse or family is very central to a worker's success. Everything I do in regard to employee recognition includes family and spouses. Why? When people do well at demanding jobs, there is almost certainly a lot of sacrifice going on at home. If a worker's home life falls apart, their performance is going to suffer dramatically. In a conventional business environment, there's a tendency to see such a person in one dimension, as someone who simply couldn't "keep it together." That's why including the family view is essential to any leader who wants to inspire loyalty. And you have to include the family view all the time, not just when things get tough. When workers succeed, the recognition and rewards need to be extended to everyone who sacrificed—including the people who seldom show up at the office.

Pull for Each Other

There were few who gave the recent American Women's Expedition to the Antarctic much chance of success. Sunniva Sorby and her three companions, explorers Anne Bancroft, Sue Giller, and Anne Dal Vera, wanted to become the first women to ski to the South Pole. It would require more than sixty days and 700 miles of very tough sledding, enduring temperatures as cold as 50 degrees below zero and winds up to 100 miles an hour. The journey would require ten-hour days, seven days a week, uphill over a bitterly alien landscape of snowdrifts and treacherous crevasses. Each team member would be in charge of pulling her own 200-pound sled. On January 14, 1993, they made history as the first women's team to reach the South Pole without the aid of sled dogs or motorized vehicles.

Those are the facts. The inside story is even more remarkable: four human beings struggling together for weeks against tough odds and dreadful conditions in the least hospitable environment on the planet. Even on their best day, pulling for all they were worth, the four women didn't quite cover fifteen miles. Each of them dealt with the effects of the bitter Antarctic climate:

frostbite, sunburn, windburn, bronchitis, and blisters. Sunniva experienced not only severe bronchitis but tendinitis as well, so much that after the excruciating pain of pulling on her frozen ski boots one morning, she discovered she could not even walk. Luckily, she found that she could still ski.

How does the impossible become the possible? According to Sunniva, it's teamwork rather than individual heroics that counts on a tough expedition. Everything depends on the emotional balance: making the day's distance quota, getting tents set up and taken down efficiently, even preparing food well. Tending to the team's emotional balance is often a matter of giving moral support and reviving teammates' enthusiasm even when one feels totally depleted of personal resources.

At one point near the end of the trip, the relentless hardship and sensory deprivation had become so severe that one member of the team plunged into depression and threatened to head off across the icy wasteland never to be seen again. Despite their own conditions of mental and physical bankruptcy, the members of the team rallied to the support of the woman most in danger. I asked Sunniva where she found the strength to help her companion when she was suffering so much herself. She related how unknown reserves of energy were tapped when members of the team shifted their focus from managing their own energy to pulling for each other:

I honestly thought I had nothing to give. It was the equivalent of a person who works an eighty-hour week and then just shuts off. So I had to let go of thinking about the South Pole and our chances of success. I let go of everything. I told myself, "What is happening right now is that this person is having trouble and she needs me. Now." It was an incredible transition for me to let go of my suffering and my attitude of "woe is me." Being forced to let go of your own pain to contribute to something larger than yourself gives you an incredible amount of strength.

Give Up the Goal

Paradoxically, giving up the goal is sometimes the key to attaining it. As Sunniva puts it:

> When you give up your attachment to reaching a specific goal, you become more of a contributor to the whole. And that's what helps bring about a successful outcome. You become more willing to share another's load. On our expedition, we didn't always carry 200 pounds apiece. Sometimes one of us could only manage 180 so another person would carry 220. The same went for the emotional load; when one person couldn't take it anymore, another team member took on the struggle for both of them.
>
> We were in an environment with no reminders of the outside world whatsoever. Within that isolated environment we were just four women who cared about each other. What is remarkable is that all the tough times reinforced the fact that we cared about each other. We didn't just say that we did, we actually did. When I look back, six years later, that's the thing I feel most proud of. We really did work to stay friends and work together as a team. Sometimes you have to give up yourself to give of yourself. And that's what we did.

Grow Invisible

Over the last few years of consulting with hundreds of organizations, I've observed that every healthy, optimally effective corporate culture has at least one exceptional example of team-oriented leadership at the top level. These individuals model full effort, an openness to new information, and a genuine concern for fellow workers. Not surprisingly, the corporate environment around these individuals tends to demonstrate those same traits. People at every level are motivated to put forth an incredible effort, inspired by a genuine emotional connection to the organization and a sense of adventure about the possibilities of the road ahead.

Included in this style of leadership is a healthy respect for the power of recognition. Leaders of successful expeditions gradually stop taking the lead and start sharing both responsibility and credit. Having given their best effort and having faith in the overall process, they gradually melt into the group so that a newcomer might not spot the leader right away. Ultimately, give-it-all-you've-got leadership lightens the load of the leader and turns everyone into a hero.

This model of leadership is hardly a New Age idea; in fact, it is as *old* age as you can get. Lao-tzu, the Chinese philosopher-sage of the sixth century B.C., described a leader who is acclaimed by the public as being *not so good*. A good leader is one who people hardly know exists. According to Lao-tzu, under the guidance of a great leader, when the job is done, people say only, "We did this ourselves."

Practice Mind Coaching

Perhaps the most visible example of a team that has benefited as a result of give-it-all-you've-got leadership is the five-time NBA champions, the Chicago Bulls, as led by basketball phenomenon Michael Jordan and former coach Phil Jackson to three consecutive titles. Behind the scenes, a man who was responsible for at least some of that success is George Mumford, the spiritual counselor and meditation guru who spent several years working and traveling with the legendary team.

Along with his one-on-one "mind coaching"—helping individual players access the mental state required to perform at the highest levels—George persuaded the entire Bulls team to meditate together, inducing a stronger sense of genuine teamwork even in the strongest personalities. According to George, "Amazing things can happen when you can get a group of guys to give up their selfish concerns and get interested in the needs of other individuals. Then you come to understand that the whole is greater than the sum of its parts."

From this kind of team understanding evolved a natural leader. "This team could easily have been nothing more than Jordan and the Jordannaires," George reflects. "But with Michael as the leader, they truly became the Bulls. If you look at their development, you see one unusually effective player coming to recognize that self-sacrifice benefits the team as a whole. Another way to say it is that Michael learned how to pass the ball. As talented as he is as an individual, it's really Michael's understanding of the entire team that made him great."

Find the Intuitive Edge

George Mumford helped the Chicago Bulls tune into the intuitive capacities of heightened consciousness, introducing them to the idea that mastering the game begins with mastering the mind. He compares the tendency to lose oneself in the thick of a game to the thrill of finding oneself atop the summit on a hard climb. "The salient question is, 'Where is your mind?'" he challenges. "You can be so moved by getting things done that you don't give yourself the time to feel what it is like to just experience the moment. You need to be present in that moment so that you can see what needs to be done next and make the most strategic move."

George uses a variety of focusing techniques. "Sitting together for prolonged periods helps team members connect in an intimate way. The point is to train the mind so it becomes focused and there is less reactivity. Some of the exercises involve sitting quietly with eyes closed in meditation. Others require some movement, such as traditional Chi Gung, which coordinates the hand and the breath."

I asked George how he has helped strong personalities overcome ego and begin giving to each other as a team.

There are some general principles but no set formula. Making individuals into a team is a process that takes a long time. First a person has to look at himself and how he relates to himself and others. He has to start seeing connections between his individual needs and the needs of the group. Then you have to have someone—in this case, the coach—who can remind everyone that ultimately they want to connect to something bigger than themselves. That's the vision from which teamwork derives. The coach has to get buy-in of that vision from his captain and the leaders of the team. Buy-in means commitment. With the team's commitment, the coach then has to communicate not just what the vision is, but how everyone is going to help make it happen. For a team to win, everybody has to buy into the vision, not just the star or strongest players.

Create a Generous Reality

If you are stingy with life, you will find yourself in the center of a stingy universe. Generosity of spirit produces an entirely different reality. The payoff of "extreme giving" is that you can win every time. When outcomes are uncontrollable despite our best efforts, we must find satisfaction in our efforts themselves. To stake our happiness on the vagaries of the market or the caprices of some rascal in the head office is a recipe for fear and self-loathing. The magic of giving all you've got and more is that success as you've defined it is guaranteed. When we've given all we've got, there is no room for regret, only delight.

The *achachilas* who run the show on the world's highest inland sea gave me a renewed faith in life as a collaborative effort with magic and unseen forces.

Make Your Own Adventures

1. PRACTICE TRAVELING LIGHT

Giving all you've got requires leaving behind what you don't need and then giving up some of what you think you do need. When you explore unknown territory, the capacity to travel light is even more important than being well provisioned. Had Nevada and I not left much of our landlubber's gear on the shores of Titicaca, our increasingly sodden craft would have sunk long before we could have completed the voyage of the sun gods. Likewise, we had to jettison our fears and doubts about our own capacities. If we had remained convinced that we didn't know how to sail, we never would have learned how! Regardless of the undertaking, adventure is jump-started as soon as we begin pitching overboard the clutter of old ideas and habits in order to make room for fresh inspiration and innovation.

Here is an invaluable exercise to help streamline your journey toward personal success by lightening your load:

> *Make a list of all the old habits that, although once useful, now waste your time and get in the way of your most adventurous vision. Write these habits down on a piece of paper. Acknowledge them, thank them like old friends for the purposes they once*

served—then burn the paper and visualize your old ways of being disappearing with the smoke. Repeat this ritual as many times as necessary to inaugurate a new way of being.

What is your most adventurous vision? Create in your mind the idealized vision of yourself, the best you imaginable, five years in the future. Imagine yourself getting on and off planes headed to an important meeting, sitting at a desk in your home office finishing up a best-seller, or fit and bronzed in a single kayak heading down a wild river in New Zealand. Or see yourself strolling down a tree-lined boulevard with your loving partner and your newborn slumbering snugly in the backpack on your shoulders. Whatever your highest vision of yourself and your life may be, concentrate on it.

Now try to come up with a list of at least five habits, attitudes, or well-worn responses that get in the way of your future vision, regardless of how useful or comforting they may have been in the past. In our culture, the usual suspects are habits like smoking, physical inactivity, junk food, too much TV watching or web surfing, and so on. Whatever the old patterns, make a note of them, give them their due, then burn them up. You will soon feel your load lightening and your velocity increasing as you simplify your life from within.

2. PRIME THE PUMP

We lacked many things on Titicaca but never liquid. We just dipped our cups and drank deeply from the clear, cold waters. Although the process is hardly discernible to the human eye, a deep lake like Titicaca must be constantly emptying in order to be replenished by fresh water. In the same way, creating space in your life for the new requires letting go of the old. "An open hand can receive more than a closed fist," is a Mapuche Indian saying. Just as the Aymara of Titicaca proffered their most prized belongings to the local gods, Native Americans have always given the spirits their most valued possessions. An offering isn't really a gift unless it represents a genuine sacrifice; it's got to hurt, just a bit, to prove you mean it. Painful as it was to part with their favorite possessions, my Native American friends tell me it still seems like a small deal to trade a plug of tobacco, or even your best blanket, if it primes the pump and ushers you into the mysterious, circular flow of life.

> *Practice giving away some things you value—without the expectation of anything in return. See what happens.*

Organize your own version of the Native American *giveaway ritual.* Clean out your closet and give away whatever you have not worn in the last six months. Make "not hoarding" a practice. Gracefully letting go of possessions returns you to the natural flow of life, as things should flow from places of higher concentration to lower. If someone is in need of something you own, why not let them have it? Surprise a friend, workmate, relative, or someone living on the streets with an impromptu gift.

Since time often seems to be our scarcest commodity, we tend to hoard it for ourselves. Here's a radical idea: Give some of your time away. Take a couple of holiday mornings to work in a soup kitchen. Volunteer for a charitable organization. Create open space in your calendar by giving up a football game or round of golf. Instead, help a colleague move, visit a sick relative, make something for a friend, write a thank-you note. Do what will make someone else feel good. Notice the way you feel, too.

3. LET YOUR LIGHT SHINE ON SOMEONE ELSE

The journals and field reports of daring undertakings reveal a surprising fact: the primary reason that expeditions fail is neither bad weather nor dangerous circumstances but out-of-control egotism. Hearty, individualistic adventurers are often their own worst enemies. What destroys expeditions are not snowstorms or typhoons but arrogant leaders and overly competitive partici- pants suffering from poor communication skills. (If you've spent a career in corporate life, these problems may sound familiar!) Here's a priceless key to developing the kind of aptitude that will do more than anything else to keep your most important under- takings on track:

> *Take time to make someone else look good. Without seeking credit for yourself, arrange for a colleague's reward or recogni- tion or work to ensure a positive outcome for the project of a peer. Take an active interest in someone else's success—without taking over. Become a mentor, guide, or anonymous supporter. Then do it again; make it a new habit. Over time, you will notice a dis- tinct improvement in your working environment.*

Recent studies show that generosity really is contagious. Recip- ients of magnanimity tend to become magnanimous. When it comes to good will and altruism in a finite social structure such as a work environment, what we send around must keep going around till it winds up where it started. And that's good for everybody.

During the last few years of working with Fortune 100 com- panies in designing programs and instructing employers and employees in team building, communication, and creativity, I've observed that while a healthy sense of competition can guaran- tee maximum market share and optimize innovation, that same drive can do tremendous harm within an organization. By shining your light on others, you can covertly subvert the kind of intra- group, ego-driven competition that can sink any kind of profes- sional expedition.

So when forward progress seems halted by strained relations in your company, your unit, or even your family, take the time to reestablish an atmosphere of contribution and appreciation. In the heat of a crisis, giving all you've got and more may seem like a dangerous extravagance —but it may also be the only way to realign everyone's energies and get things moving again.

Work Some Magic

If you take any activity, any art, any discipline,

any skill, take it and push it as far as it will go,

push it beyond where it has ever been before,

push it to the wildest edge of edges,

then you force it into the realm of magic.

—TOM ROBBINS

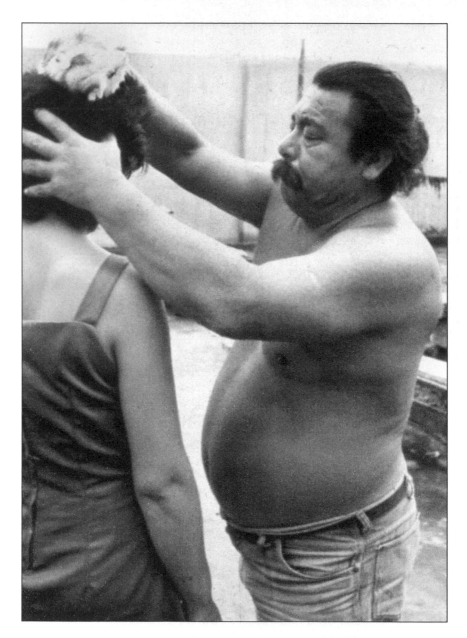

Eduardo Calderón, Wizard of the Four Winds

CHAPTER 7

The Shaman's Apprentice

My mom sewed my black velvet cape, my dad helped me print business cards. VALINI THE MAGNIFICENT, they read—"Children's Parties, Special Events, Bar Mitzvahs." At age eleven I was captivated by magic: the mystical techniques by which mere mortals could make the impossible happen. My infatuation inspired a weekly pilgrimage to Mecca Magic in East Orange, New Jersey, where the goateed store manager wowed me with incredible feats of sleight of hand. Coins passed through solid objects, silks vanished and reappeared, champagne bottles switched places, and elegantly painted Chinese boxes revealed wonder after wonder.

Even more amazing was the fact that I, Puffy Salz, could also work the magic and confound my friends and family. Unfortunately, the spiritual cost far exceeded the dollar value of the mechanical devices required to work the illusions; I fell into disenchantment when I realized that magic was mere trickery. Seeming miracles were performed by mechanics, misdirection, and artful maneuvering. For the trick to work, someone must be fooled, not enlightened.

Years passed. Wandering the jungles and mountains of the planet, I gradually became reintroduced to magic in anthropological terms. I met medicine men among the Hopi, yatiris in Nepal, *curanderos* in the hills of Guatemala and Mexico. These were men and women who were reputed to have psychic powers and an arcane knowledge of medicinal plants that induced healing. They lived in primitive societies—primitive not in the sense of "backward" but rather in the original sense of being earliest or first.

Magic returned to my world with the striking possibility that our untapped human potential lies less in what we have to invent than in what we need to remember. Wondering if the journey into the future might follow in the footsteps of those who still practiced the hidden arts of the past, I began to pursue a study of shamanism.

The Shape-Shifter

Anthropologists have found a cultural constant in traditional cultures from Siberia to the Upper Amazon. No matter the geography or social structure, inevitably there is a member of the community whose job is to act as the go-between between worlds—a shape-shifter who is in the tribe but not of it. To this individual falls the tasks of healing the sick and injured, as well as conjuring visions of possible futures for the tribe.

It is the job of the shaman to access the insights and wisdom not available to most people, who must focus their attention on the critical yet mundane demands of survival. But the shaman knows both the world of spirit and the world of flesh, and he or she is constantly watching how the realm of formlessness influences every form. The fact that this spiritual function appears to have developed independently in virtually every society and among far-flung indigenous tribes that could have had no con-

ceivable contact with each other indicates that the shaman performs an essential role in human society.

Ever since I returned from Titicaca, my daily life had been
feeling pretty constricted. My full-time job at the university had
become a repeating cycle of attendance-taking, testing, and eval-
uation. After scintillating presentations of ideas from guests like
Gary Snyder or Paul Brenner, a hand would shoot up, followed
by the anxious question: "Will this be on the exam?" An early
instinct began stirring within me again, now informed by the
curiosity of an anthropologist: Could I learn to perform real
magic without the assistance of painted boxes and hidden com-
partments? How did one become a shaman? Where did I apply?

One day my mentor Philip Staniford told me of a recent seminar at San Diego's Museum of Man where Eduardo Calderón, a
traditional Spanish-speaking shaman/healer from Trujillo, Peru,
had been invited to speak. According to Philip, whose grasp of
many languages did not include Spanish, the meeting had started
slowly with a translator struggling valiantly to present Señor
Calderón's eclectic ideas on ancient Andean shamanic principles
like energy fields, spiritual transmissions, and out-of-body travel
to a contemporary English-speaking audience. It was obvious
that worlds were being lost in the translation until, as Philip
related, "things began to flow" and Calderón's message came
across with crystalline clarity. Strangely enough, the translator
had stopped speaking entirely. Had there been some kind of
mystical transmission during a brown-bag lunch? I was not convinced.

Soon I met with Dr. Douglas Sharon, director of San Diego's
Museum of Man and sponsor of Eduardo Calderón's visit.
Sitting behind his impressive desk at the museum's executive
offices, a seemingly sober and scientific Sharon confirmed
Philip's wild report word for word. Now I was beginning to be
intrigued.

It turned out that Doug Sharon, like myself, had left home at the age of sixteen, looking for adventure. He wound up in Peru, hooking up with the legendary explorer Gene Savoy. Years of walking, machete in hand, and hacking through dense jungle culminated in the discovery of the fabled Vilcabamba, final stronghold of the Incas. Later on, through his work in indigenous healing practices on the coast of Peru, Doug Sharon obtained his Ph.D. from UCLA.

While I was teaching at San Diego State, Doug became a frequent guest lecturer. In his documentary on Eduardo Calderón, "Wizard of the Four Winds," the shaman was shown in action, diagnosing a patient's illness by passing a guinea pig over her body, skinning the guinea pig, and pulling the still-beating heart from the animal's body to determine the nature of the illness. Later in the film, healer and patient alike were seen pouring a concoction that included black tobacco and hallucinogenic cactus juice down their noses as the healing ritual proceeded. Students were shocked but mesmerized.

The techniques were certainly unorthodox, but according to Sharon they were very effective. Over the years he had witnessed a multitude of patients, now healed of their respective maladies, returning to offer their appreciation to Eduardo. His successes were gaining such notoriety that film crews had begun to arrive from places like Harvard Medical School to document his work.

One day Doug casually remarked that he thought Eduardo Calderón and I would naturally get along. "You know, if you are ever down that way, you ought to pay Eduardo a visit." Without thinking, I told Doug that the only thing standing in my way was the rest of the semester's classes. He penned a letter of introduction and sent it to Eduardo. When the last class was finished and the last paper graded, I was Peru bound. I wanted to investigate the rumors of real magic myself.

Fuzzy Latin music blared from dingy speakers as sweaty bodies jostled one another. The local bus from Trujillo to Las Delicias, Peru, was more like a contact sport than a form of transportation. The scene degenerated from paved road and glass storefronts to dirt road and adobe. In the hour it took to reach the fishing village of Las Delicias, I was journeying a decade or two backward in time. Naked children stood in the courtyards of crumbling homes, staring at the strange sight of the backpack-laden gringo. The sun beat down mercilessly.

I first saw Eduardo Calderón standing in the backyard of the ramshackle house that was both the family home and local restaurant. There was no mistaking his sumo-wrestler figure, long black hair pulled back into a ponytail, and immense bare belly extending well over the unbuttoned waistline of faded jeans. Looking more Hell's Angel than healer, he held the rapt attention of the crowd.

And quite a crowd it was, too: a fair-skinned woman in a skimpy bathing suit, straw hat, and high-top sneakers; a man in a pair of cutoff shorts, sports coat, and baseball cap; another man in a tie-dyed tank top, striped bell-bottoms, and cowboy boots.

All were snapping photographs as Eduardo, with practiced ease, passed the guinea pig over the body of a young woman, then skinned it and rinsed it under running water as he removed the innards. Squinting into the sun, he studied the glistening guts carefully as a video crew closed around him, zooming in on the action.

Facing the camera, Eduardo methodically studied the guinea pig's entrails. Closing his eyes and clenching his fists, he stood alone in the center of the sweltering courtyard. Heavy drops of perspiration rained down his face and chest. "You have a significant growth in the large intestine," he stated matter-of-factly.

Tears streamed down the woman's face. Eduardo's guinea pig rite had approximated the diagnosis she had received in Los Angeles only a week before.

A dangerous tumor—cancerous, malignant, and rapidly metastasizing—had been discovered in her intestine, she reported.

Eduardo took a step closer and held out his hand to the woman. She held on to it tightly. "Tumor, cancerous, malignant, metastasizing . . . these words are powerful," he said, pronouncing each one with dramatic disdain. "The words frighten you and can cause you to grow worse. I sense that it is fear within your body—fear that has caused this disease."

"Is there anything you can do?" sobbed the woman, her voice barely audible.

"We can give you your confidence back. I do not sense that it is too late. It is quite likely you can be healed. In five days' time we will have the full-moon ceremony. We will do all we can," he said.

The ragtag assembly murmured in awe as Eduardo washed his hands and smiled for the cameras. I had already learned my first lesson from Eduardo: To be a shaman, it helps to be a showman.

The bus I rode into Las Delicias departed with a belch of exhaust, and Eduardo invited me into his home, a single-story adobe painted turquoise. His teenage daughter Chepa, one of fourteen Calderón children, brought us beer; I could see that she had inherited the easy laughter and mischievous, knowing eyes of her famous father. Eduardo and I sat at a battered linoleum kitchen table in a room where the walls were lined with saints, family photos, and shelves of books. The air was hot in my nostrils; there was no hint of a breeze in the house. We shoveled down plate after plate of spicy potatoes, accelerating the beads of sweat rolling from my brow into my eyes. Flies were dive-bombing into my ears and hair.

"Of course there is a difference between the forces people call white magic and black magic," Eduardo was saying as I struggled to focus on something other than the insects. "Black magic is most often a product of envy, caused by socioeconomic differences or hatred between families. Evil energies are transmitted by using an article of the victim's clothing or even a photograph. The thing is, whoever causes an evil spell will ultimately be the recipient of one even worse. But white magic has only positive outcomes."

Eduardo was now fifty-three years old. In his teens, he had left his home in Trujillo to become a priest. Three years later he heard a different call and entered the School of Fine Arts in Lima. Later he returned home to study the ancient art of the Mochi and Chan Chan culture. He opened his own shop and built up a successful business creating authentic archaeological replicas in wood, stone, and ceramic. Eduardo was also experienced as a professional fisherman and dockworker and represented Trujillo as a champion weightlifter in national competitions. But there was still more to his résumé: he was a certified nurse, a black belt in judo, a poet, and a linguist of ancient languages. His bookshelves were lined with the works of Einstein, Jung, Ouspensky, and Rilke.

Eduardo had certainly paid his dues; his shamanic induction matched the archetypal legend step by step. In 1951, his body from his right shoulder to his left foot had begun to ache and swell. Soon he was in such serious pain he could no longer move. Local hospitals and physicians were useless. Eduardo sought the assistance of doña Rosa Larender Pardo, an indigenous woman of the northern coast of Peru who, according to Eduardo, was conversant with both white and black magic and had an encyclopedic knowledge of curative plants. She cured him in two days. Within forty-eight hours, Eduardo, who had been "too weak to pick up a small stone," made a total recovery. "I decided at that moment to dedicate myself to the study of the esoteric," he told me.

Eduardo pounded his beer on the table with a loud slam and gave me a challenging glare. "So you think you met the *achachilas*, eh? What did you see? Were their energies white or black?"

"I didn't see anything," I replied dumbly. "The winds and swells just changed suddenly. Maybe the *achachila* energy is bigger than that. Bigger than black or white. All I know is, I felt like a rubber duck in God's bathtub."

"*Bueno! Bueno!* Like a rubber duck in God's bathtub!" Eduardo laughed heartily and pounded me on the back. His mood was immediately lighter. Apparently, I had just passed muster and was now being ushered into the brotherhood of the unseen forces. He invited me to stay in his house.

The Shaman Within

"Not every medicine man is a shaman, but a shaman might be a medicine man," says Serge Kahili King in his book *Urban Shaman*. "Not every tribal priest is a shaman but a shaman might be a tribal priest. Not every psychic healer is a shaman but a shaman might be a psychic healer. . . . I define a shaman as a healer of relationships: between mind and body, between people, between people and circumstances, between humans and Nature, and between matter and spirit."

In an interview in *LA Weekly*, Terence McKenna, ethnopharmacologist and self-proclaimed "inner-space explorer," suggested,

> Through the ability to cure, the shaman can confer psychological wholeness on the people who come to him with problems. He is like a superhuman person, simply by virtue of the fact that he is together, he is not confused. He knows when to hang on and when to let go. . . . The shaman may appear to be a member of the culture, but he's broader, deeper, higher and wider than the culture that created him.

The shaman is a shape-shifter, moving between worlds in which others remain stuck, limited by the strict confines of their own courage and imagination. The shaman performs the role of cultural revolutionary, protagonist of the hero's journey, traveling beyond traditional mores and bringing back from the wilderness the balms and salves to ease the pains of his or her comrades.

In traditional societies, the shaman-to-be starts life on the same trajectory as anyone else. The shaman's calling, or herald, appears in a number of ways. In Native American Plains societies, it usually comes as a specific dream, an experience of empowerment during the obligatory, ritualized vision quest. While most return with a vision of their adult role in the tribe, to a certain few come the "dream of power."

In Peru, an individual's distinction as *curandero*, or healer, does not usually become evident until he or she has almost died, returning with an awakened ability to heal others. The common elements in every shaman's pilgrimage are an initial but total separation from normal life, a harrowing, often life-threatening passage that grants unusual powers, and a return home, usually to share his or her new skills with the community.

The odyssey is no cakewalk. As Igjugarjuk, the Caribou Eskimo shaman interviewed by the Danish explorer Knud Rasmussen in the early 1920s explained, "The only true wisdom lives far from mankind, out in the great loneliness, and can be reached only through suffering. Privation and suffering alone open the mind of a man to all that is hidden to others."

A week passed. One morning, I rose at dawn to bring an early end to the ceaseless encounter with ants, mosquitoes, and other mysterious biting creatures that turned every night inside my sleeping bag into a pitched battle. Rubbing eyes and a thousand itches, I shuffled out into the predawn light. An immense sea lion was stranded on the shore. Vulnerable and hurt, the animal lay beached and ailing. I approached, drawn by the labored breathing, and gazed into half-closed eyes, soft and intelligent.

A young man in an Adidas sweatshirt and thongs padded up next to me. "Oh, Dios!" he exclaimed, running off to gather his buddies. Instead of wonder, they approached with long poles, sticks, and boulders. Tossing the heavy rocks from a safe distance, they pulverized the head of the creature. Slitting the skin from throat to belly, they thrust a machete inside the body cavity and emerged with the great heart held high. Cheering, they carved him up for lunch.

Soon Eduardo returned. After playing the role of shamanic superstar for a week, he seemed pleased to be home among family and friends. The woman with the intestinal cancer had been the object of several hours of shamanic intervention in a video-recorded ritual near Machu Picchu. The ceremony, he informed me, had gone very well and the woman would be pleasantly surprised by the news she would receive after her next visit to her doctors in Los Angeles. (I checked it out later; he was right.)

Now, excited cries and bellows of laughter reverberated off cement walls as Eduardo frolicked with the smallest members of the Calderón clan. To celebrate the reunion, Chepa had found some healthy chunks of meat to adorn the nightly serving of potatoes.

"Hmm, tasty," I remarked, wolfing down rapid forkfuls of welcome protein. "Beef?"

"Oh, no. *Lobo del mar!*" She smiled sweetly. Sea lion. As I recalled those liquid, inquiring, all-too-human eyes, my throat constricted to the diameter of a dime. As my stomach clenched, I pushed the offending plate as far across the table as possible.

With a large guffaw, Eduardo reached out and lifted the meat from my plate into his own. "There is no tragedy in death, my friend," he said. "The only tragedy is a life that is wasted. We eat and are eaten. The chore of the superior man is to swallow as much of life as he can hold. That way you are the best food for the one whose job it is to eat you." He pushed my half-emptied plate back in my direction. "Eat, amigo. Do someone else a favor."

So I ate my potatoes while chewing over my host's words, wondering what I should do in order to make sure the life I had seen in the soft eyes of the sea lion was not wasted.

The Shaman's Apprentice

The next few weeks, if not magical, at least passed more quickly. At night I was still bug bait, tossing and tortured until dawn; the days were more amenable. I was pleased to discover that my Spanish language skills had improved enough that I could assist Eduardo by translating for the occasional foreign visitor and help screen the endless stream of locals who appeared at his front door every morning during official visiting hours. Although many desperately sought to make an appointment for a healing ceremony, an equal number came simply to express gratitude.

Toting bags of chickens and loaves of fresh bread, car parts and flowers, everyone told different stories with similarly welcome results. Bad luck was over; disastrous relationships had been healed; missing jewelry had been located; chronic pain was alleviated. One man had found relief from the hiccups that had tormented him for two years. For three weeks, every letter from a physician, every list of lab results or CAT scans plunked down on that beer-stained card table on Eduardo's veranda told the same story: a visit with the Wizard of the Four Winds had worked wonders.

During afternoons, after the stream of guests had dwindled, the two of us would sit down for lengthy philosophical discussions lubricated by ample amounts of *cerveza* and the ultrahigh-octane local specialty, *pisco*. At night there were family and neighborhood fiestas: birthdays, christenings, and saints' days. Watching his impressive frame move smoothly to the tinny rhythms of a small radio, I discovered yet another skill: Eduardo danced the hottest cumbia in Las Delicias.

Eduardo made a habit of partying heavily but heading home early. By ten o'clock he was always asleep; by four o'clock the next morning he was up again. "Between four and six is when the real work is done. It is when the veil between worlds is the thinnest," he explained.

A few days before my departure, the long-awaited opportunity to observe an actual ceremony arrived. The party was BYOG—Bring your own guinea pig—Eduardo announced one day over lunch.

Tuesday afternoon, the day before I was to leave, I waited outside Eduardo's workshop, guinea pig in hand. Let the magic begin.

Although the healing ceremony does not begin till long past midnight, the preparatory cleansing with guinea pig takes place in broad daylight the day before. Eduardo washed his hands, then I gave him the squirming animal. He rubbed it on my body, this way and that. He held it on my head and I felt its warmth on my scalp. All the while, Eduardo was chanting. He opened the body cavity with a penknife and held the entrails and still-beating heart under a spigot of streaming water.

"Why the water?" I asked.

"The water is the magnetic conductor that joins our energy: yours, mine, and the animal's," he explained, holding up a piece of innards for my examination. "Look, there is a stain on the lungs."

"My lungs are fine," I protested.

"Yes, perhaps nothing to worry about. It is up to you," he said quietly, and headed off to his workshop to begin preparations for the evening to come.

That night by the ocean, in the lee of a cement wall, Eduardo had organized his primary tool, the *mesa*. On a board covered with cloth lay a strange collection of diverse objects: figurines of Jesus on the cross, the Virgin Mary, and a few saints; oddly shaped stones and a variety of seashells; the foot of a deer, daggers, bones; and tiny bottles of cheap perfume and an Inca Cola bottle containing plants and floating pieces of animals. There was also a plaster statue of a mustachioed man sitting in a chair and smoking a cigar.

Standing upright in the dirt, impressively lined before the *mesa*, was an array of staffs and swords. They lent the immediate area the quality of a battlefield. Something was about to happen, and it would not be a softly lit New Age ritual involving crystals and unicorns. The *mesa* contains both dark and light elements because it is a game board where the shaman "plays out" in microcosm the battle between life and death, good and evil. The ritual is gritty, unnerving, and profoundly real.

Eduardo described the *mesa* as a kind of "receiver-transmitter" for unseen energies: "Like a radio. A radio is no more than an arrangement of glass tubes and wires and empty space in a box. Yet when in proper alignment, in proper relationship, they can draw unseen music from the air or send your voice to corners of the world. This principle is identical to the way the items of a *mesa* work."

Seated behind the low *mesa*, Eduardo chanted, shook rattles, and used his mouth to spray explosions of home-brewed alcohol to the four directions. The cornmeal circle before him was empty; it was not yet midnight. The *mesa* was still being "opened." A dozen of us huddled together for warmth, waiting.

At midnight the first patient, a young Trujillo man dressed in a light poncho and worn-out tennis shoes, was invited to enter the circle. One leg twisted, noticeably an inch or two shorter than the other, he grimaced in pain as he shuffled forward. He was no more than twenty-five years old. His cheeks showed a light stubble and his eyes were wide and uncertain. One of Eduardo's two attendants approached with a shallow silver bowl bearing a concoction of San Pedro cactus mixed with sacred herbs, perfume, and tobacco juice. With the attendant's help, the contents disappeared down the young man's nose. First one nostril, then the other.

Eduardo then pulled a rusted bayonet from the ground and handed it to the young patient, who was now shaking slightly, with eyes half-closed. Eduardo's chant invoked a pantheon of spirits from Santa Maria to Simón Bolívar. Waves crashed onto the pebble beach as sparks from the fire rose high into the sky. Hunched over on his seat, fists clenched on his thighs, Eduardo stared unblinking at the man for many minutes. The healer's eyes, reflecting the fire, were as fierce as a hawk's.

I listened as Eduardo described the young man's aura. "Pain. Much pain," he intoned. "A woman you have angered. A woman you have hurt. And now you are suffering as well."

"Yes," whispered the man, his eyes now open, rolling back in his head.

"You have sores, no? You are weak, cannot sleep? Depressed, no?"

"Yes. Yes."

"And that leg. It has shriveled and is hurting. How long?"

"A couple of months…."

"It is *el mal ojo*. This woman has found a way to surround you with evil. But the power of good is stronger." Eduardo had risen from the bench, his bulk a powerful presence beneath his poncho. His muscular arms glistened in the orange light of the flames as he pulled a sword from the dirt. His other hand held the mystery bottle of herbs and animal chunks from which he filled his bulging cheeks. He turned to the four cardinal directions, spitting mouthfuls of the liquid into the black night. Refilling his mouth, he approached the young man and doused him from head to toe with spray.

Returning the bottle to the *mesa*, he scanned the young man from head to toe, finally alighting on a spot a few inches above his head. He motioned with his sword, as if inviting an unseen adversary into battle. Then, with an agility shocking for a man of his size, he leaped repeatedly into the air, his sword glinting and flashing like a blade of flame.

Retaking his seat, Eduardo sat in silence, eyes closed, chest heaving. Finally, he opened his eyes and turned again to the young man who was now trembling uncontrollably. "Step through the fire. Hold the sword high. You will step four times. Like this." Eduardo motioned with his hand. The man stepped slowly, deliberately through the middle of the fire, flames licking at his poncho, miraculously untroubled.

Thus was *el mal ojo* overcome, the black spirit sent back to its home by a lake in the mountains. The young man must pay better attention to his relationships, explained Eduardo; he must right any wrong he has done, then change his habits and take certain herbs.

The fellow was smiling as the ritual drew to a close, saying he was feeling good. As he turned confidently away from the cornmeal circle I noticed that he was no longer limping. He covered the ten feet back to his place on the spectator's bench in long, easy strides. I checked my watch; the bizarre process had taken half an hour.

One by one, the patients took their place before the *mesa*. An old country woman in a tall straw hat and black shawl had a bleeding ulcer that would not heal. A well-to-do city man in sports coat and shiny shoes was in the throes of a streak of bad luck that had already cost him his house. These afflictions, too, Eduardo attributed to black magic. He repeated, with some variations, his contests with unseen forces to send the evil energy back to its source.

Then a father shoved forward a little boy, no more than five years old. The boy's eyes were crossed, his vision impaired. Eduardo spoke bluntly of an unhappy family life. Only after the father had expressed a willingness to change his behavior toward his wife and children did Eduardo consent to work on the boy with chants, sprays of various liquids, and the manipulation of sacred objects on his *mesa*. The boy expressed that his vision was already much improved. His eyes, however, still looked crossed. "The rest is up to you," Eduardo said sternly to the father. "Anger in your heart brings dark spirits into the lives of all around you. You must fill the hole inside you for your family to be healthy again."

The hours sped by. Soon it was nearly four in the morning. Four is the time when the mesa must be closed.

"Señor Salz," Eduardo called, nodding in the direction of the fire. I hesitated, uncertain if I was really meant to participate in the ritual. I checked Eduardo's eyes; they were warm, almost humorous. He nodded and I took my place within the cornmeal circle. I felt quite vulnerable, my core entirely exposed.

The San Pedro entered my nose, poured from the lip of the silver bowl by the knowing hands of an assistant. It burned my nasal passages and stung my throat as I swallowed, involuntarily making loud, gulping sounds. As he chanted, Eduardo handed me the staff crowned with a top hat and mustachioed face: Maximón, the roguish, black-suited, stogie-puffing people's saint of Guatemala, decidedly unsanctioned by the Catholic Church. He is the protector of the uncertain, the impious, and the intemperate; the selection felt strangely familiar and appropriate. My legs trembled uncontrollably. I felt wobbly, yet somehow fearless and ecstatic. I was afraid I'd start laughing uncontrollably at any moment.

"You have walked! God, how you walk," Eduardo suddenly exclaimed. "What are you looking for?" He paused, staring deeply into my eyes. "I see you hanging to a claw-shaped mountain, hanging by a rope, struggling toward the top. But you are not supposed to be there. There is death. Someone dies but he walks beside you still. Soon you are going to lose another great teacher and friend. Too soon. You cannot cease from walking, climbing, but to no avail. You are lost, my friend." He shook his rattle as a chunk of log exploded, sparks rising in a tail of flame.

The cold night breeze, fanning the fire, chilled me to the marrow. My body trembled as Eduardo's words tumbled out. His gaze, more like that of a fierce animal than a human being, bored right through me. He was no longer my friend; he was something else, some strange being from another plane of existence. He continued his low droning, a stream of consciousness narration of the movie that seemed to be playing inside his head. I was clenching my fists and brimming with tears—I had hoped for much better news!

"Do not fear," Eduardo intoned. "Your mind and heart are expanding and soon they will be open wide. You will understand that the mountain you seek is not for climbing. It is always with you, a place for inspiration. Your life will change. I see you in rooms, many rooms full of thousands of people. You are one who holds a lantern. I will invoke the spirit of Maximón to bring you a healthy life, prosperity, and purpose. But you must keep the peace with Maximón. He wants you to share tobacco and some good *pisco*." The assistant handed me a lit cigar and I brought it to my lips for a puff.

"No, not for you!" Eduardo roared with laughter. "For him." Eduardo laughed, motioning to the end of the staff I still held in my hand. Then I blew smoke into the mouth of Maximón. I was handed a shot of fiery *pisco*, also for Maximón. Now I was the one spewing the contents of my mouth into the night air.

"Bueno," exulted Eduardo. We were done.

Shortly before dawn I sat alone on the patio. The house was dark, everyone else asleep. I felt pleased, yet also disappointed, for I had seen no life-altering vision or had any out-of-body experiences, nor had the world shifted for me in any significant way. Sure, he had pegged my past well enough for me to feel he had somehow read my mail. But maybe he had. He could have gotten information about me from our long talks, for I didn't remember everything that I had confessed.

As for Eduardo's visions of my future, I was unconvinced. Yet somehow everything seemed different. I felt remarkably vital and energized considering I hadn't slept all night.

Then I remembered something Eduardo had told me a few days earlier as we stood on the beach looking over the gray, leaden sea. "Don't be disappointed when I say this, but there is no such thing as magic. It is all right here." He tapped the side of his head. "If there is magic, it is in the laws of nature and science. Some of the laws we may not understand or even perceive yet, but they exist nonetheless. Healing is a kind of superpsychology that we approach through ritual. I help people by allowing them to believe in me so that I can help them to heal themselves." He had given me a conspiratorial wink. "The truth is, they do all the work."

Eduardo walked me to the bus stop as I tried to press a wad of pesos into his hand to help pay for some of the food, beer, and *pisco* I'd consumed in the last month. He thrust it back into my pocket. He would not accept payment, he said, for what had been given in friendship. Nor would he say good-bye.

"Men like us do not say farewell," he insisted. He clasped me to his barrel chest for one hearty hug, then turned and ambled homeward, bearlike, in the half-lit morning.

Men like us, Eduardo had said. That phrase was the incantatory gift I would take home with me, I decided. Men like us, I thought, make magic. But I was not really a man like Eduardo; not yet. I'd like to think that someday I might be.

Hacking and spitting, I took my place among the chickens, sacks of potatoes, and dried fish in the back of the bus to Trujillo. I needed to make an international call and have a friend back home wire enough money to allow me to continue my trip across Peru. The phone call delivered some shocking news.

"Didn't you know Phil Staniford in the anthro department at State?" asked my friend. "Well, the news is bad. I think he was out jogging—anyway, he had a heart attack and died right there on the street near his home."

When the money arrived, I caught the first plane home, spooking the flight attendants as I convulsed and coughed all the way from Lima to Los Angeles. The day after we scattered Philip's ashes on a sacred mountain, I was diagnosed with an infection that had lodged in my chest, requiring a week of bed rest and a rigorous dose of antibiotics.

Eduardo was also reasonably accurate about my future livelihood and location. Though I live in a mountain cabin across from Taquitz Peak and the best climbing in Southern California, I spend considerably less time scaling the neighborhood mountain than simply being inspired by its constant presence through the window of the home office where I run my professional speaking business.

What do I speak about? Lessons learned in places like Patagonia and Peru. While I am no shaman, I learned at least one lesson from my friend Eduardo: the true vocation of the awakened human being—whether shaman, speaker, or CEO—

is not acquiring personal power, but helping others to find theirs.

To this day, on the windowsill above my desk sits a figurine of the enigmatic, black-suited Maximón, a fresh Cuban cigar resting on his lap. Just in case.

CHAPTER 8

How to Make Magic

Eduardo Calderón embodied the tradition of the man of power as the individual to whom others look for healing and inspiration. But as he admitted to me, his art was in part a psychological sleight of hand that initiates the process of self-healing. In modern culture, we may turn to therapists or professional coaches for a similar kind of insight and inspiration, even if the language and techniques used seem very different.

Become Your Own Healer

If we are always dependent on others for our healing and motivation, we are cheating our own potential. The task at hand is to discover that we are all healers, creators, and shape-shifters. Becoming our own men and women of power means developing and refining the shamanic skills that make one's personal and professional life an adventure of ongoing transformation instead of a predictable routine.

The following prescription for magic translates the traditional shaman's art into a handful of manageable, pragmatic

steps that make sense today. These are also the steps to a visionary style of leadership—an inspired, constantly evolving mind-
set that looks beyond "getting the job done" toward the
transformations that are latent in present-day circumstances. In
a global business environment where the capacity to transform
your enterprise on short notice is an indispensable survival skill,
working magic is crucial.

The four elements of working magic are:

1. Find Your Vision
2. Make Your Own Meanings
3. Jump-Start Your Inner Search Engine
4. Live an Interesting Life

1. Find Your Vision

It is often said of shamans that they have "a foot in both
worlds"—the world of spirit to which they journey to find healing visions and the ordinary physical world in which they apply
their insights for the benefit of others. Malidoma Patrice Somé
is an initiated West African shaman whose life story is a remarkable adventure of straddling two very different worlds right here
on earth.

Malidoma—whose name translates roughly as "be friends
with the stranger/enemy"—was born in 1956 into the Dagara
tribe in Burkina Faso (then the French colony of Upper Volta).
Taken from his village with his father's consent by neighboring
Jesuits at age four, Malidoma was trained as one of a new gener-
ation of native missionaries. For the next sixteen years, he experienced an intensive and sometimes harsh indoctrination into the
ways of the West; his native Dagara tongue was literally beaten
out of him and replaced with French and Latin. At age twenty,

Malidoma rebelled by taking a swing at a cruel instructor and then escaping into the jungle to find his way home to his tribe. Without food or money, he walked more than a hundred miles back to his birthplace.

Once he had returned, Malidoma's own mother had difficulty recognizing him and most of the villagers eyed him with suspicion as someone hopelessly contaminated by "the wilderness"—their term for modern, Western-style culture. After a difficult year of adjustment, Malidoma's elders decided that he must go through the Dagara rite of initiation into manhood, even though he would enter the ritual seven years later than normal and without the benefit of preparation that Dagara boys usually receive for the forty-day ordeal of physical challenges, emotional and psychological surrender, and transcendental experience. Some of the tribe's elders warned that the ritual could kill Malidoma, and a few wondered aloud whether that might not be the best thing for him.

As described in his autobiography *Of Water and the Spirit*, Malidoma's initiation ritual combined the physical rigors of fasting and wandering in the wilderness with experiences that Westerners can only understand as the stuff of dreams and visions. At one point Malidoma and his young village brothers entered into the "otherworld" by jumping into a "light hole" created by the elders in the middle of a swinging cowhide. The boys' bodies dissolved and then rematerialized a few minutes later, emerging from the light hole bearing tongues of violet fire.

In Malidoma's case, the initiation ritual crystallized the destiny of "befriending the stranger/enemy" that was latent within his name. (In Dagara tradition, unborn children communicate their name and destiny to tribal elders in a prebirth ritual while the mother is in a trance state.) The elders told Malidoma that he must leave the village once more in order to be further educated in the West and become a teacher of indigenous ways to the modern world. "The village will be reborn in the heart and soul of the culture that is destroying the village," the elders told their cultural ambassador.

Malidoma returned to his formal education with a vengeance, first going to the university in Burkina Faso's capital city of Ouagadougou and then earning three master's degrees and two doctorates—one in political science from the Sorbonne in Paris and one in literature from Brandeis University. About ten years ago, he was teaching African culture at a Michigan university where he had been joined by his wife, Sobonfu (her name means "keeper of the knowledge"), when the elders informed Malidoma that a comfortable university position was not what they had in mind when they appointed him to be their cultural messenger. It was then that he began writing books and going on the road as a workshop leader teaching ritual, working with such noted visionaries as psychologists James Hillman and Michael Meade and poet Robert Bly. Today Malidoma and Sobonfu continue to teach indigenous wisdom all over the United States and Europe while helping out their homeland through a nonprofit foundation.

THE FUN OF SPIRIT

Despite the seriousness of his mission to teach the ways of the village to a modern culture that he sees as profoundly out of balance, Malidoma suggests that the best route to a healing spiritual vision is through fun. "The idea that anything spiritual must be solemn and serious is a big problem in the West," he says. "It's very hard to wake up people here to a liberated spirituality—a spirituality that allows the soul some relaxation and good feeling. In the village, people like to stay in a ritual space singing and dancing all night because it's fun. You know, the spirit within us is like a child. When the child has its proper toys, it can play."

Malidoma explains:

The toys for the spirit are the natural world, the community, a sense of purpose, and a craving to be with invisible friends. You have to play in a natural place, away from the downtown and the freeway. Your toys have to be the stones and rocks, and the creek running with pure water, and the trees. You have to be in a space that hasn't been rearranged by civilization. And you have to stay long enough to get over being homesick for the city. Then you start seeing such beauty in the trees, and the creek starts to look very interesting.

TAKE A WALK AND TUNE IN

Once you've reached that state, suggests Malidoma, tuning in to hear the voice of spirit and finding your own shamanic vision is less difficult than you might expect.

It's not complicated! You can go for a walk in nature and just watch, and listen. Someone asked me once how to hear what nature was saying, and I told him, "Just go out there, put your hand into a creek, pull out a stone and listen. You'll hear something." The important thing is not to panic when you do start hearing something and don't know whether it's for real. Give yourself the benefit of the doubt. That is what most people fail to do. They have a magical experience, and then they surround it with resistance and questioning. They will come to me and say, "I think I heard something, but I would like to know for sure." I say, "What do you mean, for sure? Let me tell you, that stone is for sure!"

FIND YOUR BLACK BOX

Modern civilization offers few initiation rituals for our youth beyond acquiring a driver's license or drinking a first beer. And we have almost completely lost the understanding of what indigenous initiation rituals are meant to provide: a sense of one's function or purpose within a community.

Malidoma Somé says the ritual experience is meant to join three fundamental aspects of human experience: self, spirit, and community. It's the lack of such initiations, he contends, that leads to problems like violence among young people, particularly in inner-city environments, where family structures are often fractured. Malidoma explains:

> Violence is a force that is trying to open up what I call an individual's black box—all the information that was stored within a soul on its journey to earth. Unless we recover that information, it's very difficult to know what our purpose is on this planet. The individual will do anything and everything to open that black box; this drive can become a very wild energy with the power to kill other people, as well as the person caught up in it. We want to put this drive away because it's scary. But our fear of violence should be a reminder that we're close to something very powerful. Violence is often an expression of the proximity of magic.

LET POWER USE YOU

Fortunately, anyone of any age can be constructively initiated to their purpose by regular returns to nature and by the kind of close listening and looking that respects the power to be rediscovered there. This is what Malidoma calls the "power of the other side," which is utilized by every kind of shaman. "This power is so huge we can't even fathom it," he warns. "We cannot own or control it; we can only serve it. To do that, one must constantly ask, 'How humble am I when I approach power?' To hold on to power, you must constantly guard against self-inflation or ego tripping. Envision yourself as servant, not proprietor, of the powers around us all. Honor their mystery. And let them use you."

USE THE POWER OF VISION

Acquiring a vision—and applying its wisdom in everyday life—is not just an exercise for individuals on a spiritual search. According to management consultant Steve Haines, the quality and power of organizational vision can change the direction of giant corporations, and even nations, for better or worse.

Founder of the Center for Strategic Management in San Diego, Haines has consulted with scores of organizations ranging from the Best Western Hotels chain and construction firm Sundt Companies, Inc., to the city governments of Yuma, Arizona, and Saskatoon, Saskatchewan, Canada, on a "Systems Thinking Approach" to planning for the future. This approach helps organizations to first develop an inspiring and practical vision and then devise and implement the strategies to achieve it. Far from being a sentimental exercise resulting in empty platitudes posted on office walls, Haines says, the development and implementation of vision is crucial to sustaining the health of an organization over time.

"Remember what happened to the senior George Bush in 1992 when he was asked about his vision and he replied, 'What's this vision thing?'" Haines remarks. "That really burned him in the election because after that people thought he was trying to win reelection as a matter of birthright. Whether they admit it or not, people are always looking for a vision of the future. Rightly or wrongly, Bill Clinton was positively associated with such a vision for a lot of people back then."

YOU NEED A VISION

In the business world around the same time, IBM was undergoing a fundamental change and hired a new CEO, Lou Gerstner. "Now he was also asked for his vision and claimed that he didn't have one," remembers Haines, adding:

He said that he didn't have time for a vision because he simply had to turn the company around as quickly as possible. In truth, Gerstner secretly had a vision that was part of his strategic plan: to turn IBM from a hardware company into a computer services company. He implemented that fundamental shift by hiring top-level consultants from major industries, such as the oil industry, to find out what kind of computer services were needed by those industries. Then he rebuilt IBM around the provision of those services. Today IBM is back on track as a fast-growth company, and over half their business profits derive from computer services. You don't transform a company that way by just increasing efficiency. You must have a vision of an ideal future and then take deliberate steps to implement it.

The lack of an effective vision can have just the opposite results, warns Haines:

Some years ago General Motors attempted a major transformation without a vision, and they're still paying for it. The CEO of that time, Stempel, announced the closing of twenty-three plants and the layoff of 76,000 people in order to balance GM's capacity with their sales. They announced proudly that the company would be "half its former size." The problem was that there was no vision associated with this cutback; it was just an efficiency move. Stempel never articulated a vision for GM's future, and he was fired in about six months. The leadership since has never really committed to a vision either, and I believe that's why their market share continues to slide. On the other hand, Ford has kept focused on their well-known vision of "Quality Is Job 1" that they formulated in the eighties, coupled with the nineties goal of outpacing GM's sales. They're achieving that goal as we speak.

Take a Mental Journey

Steve Haines admits that getting executive teams to take on the imaginative work of "visualization" is not always easy:

> Usually we take the company leaders through a guided imagery about acquiring a vision of the future. I'll have them close their eyes and do a mind's-eye journey on a supersonic transport that takes them five years into the future. They step off the plane and take a look at the ideal condition of their company and then report back on what it looks, sounds, and feels like. I call this exercise a "mental journey," and we do it while just sitting quietly at the table. Often I tell them that I don't really care whether they close their eyes to visualize, because a lot of them would get uncomfortable even doing that much. What I'd really like to do is turn off the lights, have everyone lie on the floor with their shoes off, and really do it right. But you can't go that far with an executive team. So I give them permission to leave their eyes open during their mental journey, and most of them end up closing their eyes anyway.

Shamanic visualization is getting easier for some up-and-coming executives. As a *Business Week Online* report revealed, one of the big hits of the 1999 summer convention of the Young Presidents' Organization was a "shamanic healing journey" conducted in the basement of Rome's palatial Excelsior Hotel. "There, in a candlelit room thick with a haze of incense, 17 blindfolded captains of industry lay on towels, breathed deeply, and delved into the 'lower world' to the sound of a lone tribal drum," reported *BWO*. "[The leader] instructed the executives how to retrieve from their inner depths their 'power animals' who would guide their companies to 21st-century success."

2. Make Your Own Meanings

Eduardo Calderón gave me a glimpse through the smoke and mirrors of his art when he tapped his head and said, "There is no such thing as magic. It is all right here." One very modern scientist who agrees is health researcher Dr. Margaret Kemeny, chair of the Department of Psychoneuroimmunology (PNI) at the University of California, Los Angeles. Kemeny's work centers around the study of how our mind directly affects our body's ability to battle illness. Featured in the Bill Moyers television special "Healing the Mind," she has spent the last dozen years looking at how our "belief systems" affect our immune systems.

"We have a large body of data indicating that what you expect will happen to your health is a major predictor of what usually does," says Dr. Kemeny. Citing recent research among HIV-infected people, she adds, "What we are finding is that the patients with negative expectations go on to develop AIDS and die more quickly. Their immune systems deteriorate faster, and expectation is a predictor of these immunologic changes." It appears that our beliefs about our futures directly affect our present.

Whether or not Eduardo actually interceded with spirit beings on behalf of his patients, it is likely that their belief in the healer alone would have been enough to create a positive effect. Known in the West as the "placebo effect," this phenomenon is currently the subject of much investigation. As Dr. Kemeny reports,

> We are finding that if a doctor you trust, respect, or believe in—a very authoritative source—says, "Here is a drug that is going to make you better" and gives you a placebo, then anywhere between 35 percent and 75 percent of patients get well thereafter. They show actual biological changes. We think it

is the expectation the patient develops that is facilitated by the doctor, the healer, or the shaman.

If it's how you think that matters more than what's happening to you, then treatment modalities have to change radically. In this view, the notion that stress affects health is really a misplaced idea because it says that your health is primarily impacted by something that is outside of you. The common way of thinking about it is, "Oh my God, I've got so much stress at work that it is making me sick." But it is what is going on in your head that makes a difference.

FIND MEANING IN ADVERSITY

If we think of our lives in the context of a mythic journey, even severe misfortune may be advantageous to our health. Findings show that challenging events such as losing a home to fire, losing a job, or even losing a loved one do not necessarily trigger a downturn in the immune system. But people who "bounce back" from such traumas owe their resilience to more profound states of inner optimism than the superficial determination to "turn lemons into lemonade" or "put on a happy face."

"There is a kind of optimism that is false," says Dr. Kemeny. "You may say, 'My house is burning down? Great, I'll toast marshmallows,' but that doesn't resonate with what is going on deep inside. It's when people sincerely confront dramatic experiences and manage to come out of that confrontation with a truly optimistic perspective that their health actually benefits. People who have lost someone close to them from AIDS and confronted the loss, grieving it completely, actually get a new perspective on life and greater vitality as a result. They learn to make their own meaning from adversity. That's where a genuine, healthy optimism comes from."

Eduardo's *mesa* contained elements of both light and dark; the journey to meaning passes through both sun and shadow. In the shamanic view, a time of darkness is not necessarily evil or gloomy; it represents a necessary passage through imbalance toward balance. As we begin to make our own sense of the alternating patterns of light and dark in our lives, the story line of our life starts to make sense.

Psychologist and concentration camp survivor Viktor Frankl put it this way: "There is nothing in the world, I venture to say, that would so effectively help one survive even the worst conditions as the knowledge that there is meaning in one's life." Frankl himself drew inspiration from the words of Nietzsche: "He who has the why to live for can bear almost any how."

3. Jump-Start Your Inner Search Engine

Success comes to those innovators who are able to draw together the most dissimilar concepts and ideas with the greatest ease. Visionaries, inventors, and shamans are all synthesizers par excellence, discovering fresh connections where others never think to look. That's because they're always actively looking; visionaries know how to jump-start their inner search engines on a regular basis. Searching beyond the conventional news and views of the day, they seek information from the widest possible array of sources.

LEARN INVENTIVENESS

Ralph Osterhout's mind launches ideas like a pitching machine throwing out baseballs. A slide here, a curve there, and lots of fastballs. He throws out inventions the same way. President and CEO of Machina, Osterhout oversees an enterprise that designs, engineers, and manufactures products ranging from twelve major defense systems to laser-hardened telescopes, from office systems to high-performance sporting accessories. "Inventiveness is a process that can be learned," Osterhout asserts, naming two major elements in the alchemy of creation: the broadest possible array of resources and the capacity to put them together in new ways.

Osterhout says:

> We're in an age of too many specialists. Today you hire this multimedia specialist, this medical specialist, this legal specialist, this forensic accounting specialist. There was a time when it was a noble pursuit to become a renaissance person, meaning you were well read, well spoken, physically fit, able to operate competently in many arenas of life without depending on specialists. To do that today you've got to expose yourself to a ton of information on a regular basis. That maximizes your potential to do what human beings do best: integrate disparate information and synthesize a cohesive whole.

Where does Osterhout find his wide array of information? Magazines, for one:

> Lots of them. Reading a page here and a page there, from *Business Week* to *Popular Mechanics* to *California Mining Journal.* You can cross-reference a general topic to see how it figures in all these different media. Little by little you gain a broader sense of the long-term importance of any concept. No matter how well written or cohesive a single article in *Forbes* or *Business Week* may be, you simply can't experience the same intellectual impact as you can from sampling a multiplicity of viewpoints in a variety of publications.
>
> Then you loosen your tie and put your feet up for a while, and then Eureka! All of a sudden, you've got it. You realize that the wonderful parallel processor upstairs is always trying to put together these little bits of information, and

periodically it creates something new, something magical. If you feed your mind, you'll get results.

SMELL CHANGE

Osterhout attributes his success not to his education or experience but to his willingness to change, comprising a sensitivity to shifting currents and a readiness to adjust course when necessary. "What do you think is more valuable," he challenges , "an MBA or the capacity to sense a major new trend in our culture? When you can smell change before anyone else, that's infinitely more valuable than your credentials or achievements."

Osterhout recalls how even he was caught up short by the rapid growth of the Internet.

> I remember speaking at a conference a few years ago where everyone was talking about the Internet as the next happening thing. "What the hell is the Internet?" I thought. I didn't see any immediate relevance to what I was doing. Now, of course, it's profoundly changing all our lives. The lesson for me was that if you can't reorder your thoughts and adapt rapidly to unexpected and profound transformations of your environment, you may find yourself with a skill set that has been seriously compromised by the pace of change.

4. Live an Interesting Life

Doug Sharon recognized Eduardo's uniqueness at their first meeting during an archaeological exploration in Peru. "We were collaborating with Eduardo's group, which was doing restorations," Sharon recalls. "The thing that fascinated me about him on that very first encounter was his joie de vivre. He had a marvelous sense of humor and a grasp of the larger reality of life without being cynical."

According to Sharon, this kind of "living large" is a core personality trait of the shaman. "Shamans have a capacity for organic, holistic thinking. They see the whole picture—all the parts of existence, including the parts that are hidden from physical view. Shamans can perceive reality in a way that transcends the limitations of the physical senses. They see the 'other side' of life, which is always right in front of our eyes, but most of us don't perceive it."

Another characteristic of healers, sages, and seers of all cultures is their wide range of interests and experiences. "They are real renaissance men and women," says Sharon. "These people have rich family lives and relationships with friends and colleagues. They are usually multimedia artists; Eduardo, for instance, sculpted in stone, clay, and wood, and spent some time painting. In simpler societies, at the tribal level, shamans are usually the singers, poets, and storytellers. And they usually have a well-developed sense of humor. In general, shamans are well-rounded individuals involved in daily life at a great depth."

Can ordinary humans access and develop shamanic powers? No and yes, says Doug Sharon. "Shamanism is a life's work, a calling for which only a small handful are truly gifted." Yet Sharon recalls Eduardo talking about the vista, the capacity for extraordinary vision. "Eduardo would say that vision is accessible to all. Everyone has this potential, but developing it takes discipline and hard work. You can't spend a weekend with some charismatic teacher and come back enlightened; you've got to work at it your whole lifetime."

The discipline begins with the willingness to live adventurously. Our painting is only as rich as our palette, our poetry only as lyrical as our lives. All we have to draw from is the diversity of our experiences. To fulfill the shamanic job description of leaping between worlds requires firm footing on multiple planes of experience.

COLLECT SOLUTIONS FOR PROBLEMS YOU HAVEN'T HAD YET

"The key is to live an interesting life," says creativity consultant Michael Weber, who makes his living teaching imagination skills in the highly practical, production-based environment of corporate America. "To live creatively is to be constantly collecting solutions for problems you haven't yet encountered. Creativity is a lifelong practice, not a weekend hobby or a special project." A licensed attorney in California, Weber has consulted on creativity for companies as diverse as Walt Disney, the New York Times, and Microsoft.

Weber asserts that genuine magic is already a part of our daily experience. "Microchips are magical things, so are telephones and simple magnets. I'm probably one of the biggest skeptics around about otherworldly claims, but that's only because I've seen so many really remarkable things that can be explained but are still magic to me!"

Though reluctant to admit it, Weber himself is actually a wizard who's brought magic into millions of lives. He specializes in creating real-time special effects—as opposed to digitally manipulated ones—for television and film. He created the illusion of Gary Sinise's missing legs in *Forrest Gump*. Weber's discovery of a way to get into locked bags without the use of tools resulted in the Internal Revenue Service instituting a change in their security bag design.

In Weber's view, problems are not occasional challenges that must invariably be greeted with consternation and frustration; problems are the very stuff of life. "Whether you're painting or climbing Mount Everest, creativity consists of finding the most elegant means to reach a particular end. Creativity is problem-solving and problem-solving is life. So from the day we're born to the day we die, we are being creative."

Working magic begins with being "interested in everything," concludes Weber. Why? Because casting your net of curiosity as widely as possible "gives you the possibility of coming across some wonderful, strange connections. You find yourself short-circuiting between two unrelated ideas and suddenly you hit the great idea. And there is your solution."

THINK MAGICALLY

The reputation of magic in our culture has not improved much since my days as Valini the Magnificent. For most of us, the term "magic thinking" usually denotes mere superstition or a wishful delusion. But as a world-wandering anthropologist I have had the opportunity to spend a lot of time in cultures where magic is not only reputable, it is considered integral to everyday life. While I don't believe in the existence of the supernatural, I do believe there are a number of natural phenomena that supersede our ability to investigate and explain them. In its own way, shamanism is the applied science of the inexplicable—a way to use powers of consciousness that we cannot yet explain for practical and positive purposes.

Just as thinking outside the box of familiar mental models helps us find imaginative solutions to everyday challenges, so does the ability to step outside the box of our cultural mind-set help us find solutions to even larger questions, such as: What is the source of our creativity? How do we maximize our potential for genius? and How can we be prepared for a future that is ever more unpredictable?

We need to invest our whole way of thinking with a sense of magic that is inspired, sensible, and productive.

ALLOW FOR A LARGER REALITY

The first lesson of anthropology is the danger of ethnocentrism, the belief that our particular culture is the center of the universe. This awareness enlightens us to the hazards of making arbitrary judgments of good and bad, or right and wrong, based solely on the unique set of values that comprise our habitual belief system. Those judgments include the fundamental determination of what is possible or impossible, what is real and what is illusory—distinctions that we often make semiconsciously, without even stopping to question our deepest assumptions. Working magic begins with venturing beyond our habitual and consensual notions of what is real—especially because creativity and inventiveness depend on making something out of nothing, synthesizing a new reality out of what we already know and what we can only imagine.

Because we do not perceive something is not to say it does not exist. Any quantum physicist worth his or her quarks will tell you that there is precious little matter in the world that we can see; it is virtually all space and energy. The "blur" of whirring subatomic particles creates the illusion of the solid universe we perceive. Our worldview is the result of poor eyesight; the limits of our perception are obvious. We need only to tune in to our favorite FM station to be reminded that despite their invisibility, radio waves do exist.

Author and scientist Lyall Watson points out that the electromagnetic spectrum ranges in wavelength from a billionth of a centimeter to millions of miles, yet only a tiny pinpoint of this spectrum—apparently between 380 and 760 billionths of a meter—is visible to us. The vast majority of forms of energy cannot be seen with our naked eyes.

"The difference between us and Helen Keller," writes novelist Tom Robbins, "is that she knew she was blind."

Why do we see what we see? We see only what we need to survive. The frog's depth of vision is about the length of its tongue because that's where the flies are; beyond that, the frog has just enough peripheral vision to spy approaching dangers. "The difference between us and the frog is just one of degree," says author Philip Slater in his book *The Wayward Gate.*

We see a tiny fragment of reality—one that allows us to master our physical environment—and little more. Knowing how little we can see (or hear or smell, or feel or taste, or sense)—knowing how little the frog sees and why it sees what it does see—tells us something important about our understanding of reality. What we mean by reality is not what exists. Reality is merely what we need.

The realities of the world beyond our lilypads are changing as never before. The choice is ours: Do we become visionaries? Or do we just sit around the pond wondering what happened to all the flies?

Burst Your Bubbles

During a recent conversation with Doug Sharon, he mentioned Eduardo Calderón's death a few years ago from kidney failure. I was shocked. It was disconcerting to realize that a man of such great vitality, who will always be very alive in my mind, had actually passed on.

Doug recalled one of his favorite encounters with Eduardo, at a farewell party concluding one of Doug's longer stays in Peru. He and Eduardo had put away quite a few drinks when Eduardo pointed toward the beer that had been poured into a large gourd bowl resting on the table, according to local custom.

"See those bubbles?" Eduardo said, pointing to the foam on the surface of the beer. "Those bubbles are people like you and me, floating on the top of a big ocean." He popped one of the bubbles and said, "Now one of those bubbles has gone back to the sea. It was always in the sea anyway. That's the way you and I are. Therefore there's no good-bye. Let's not say farewell, because we're part of something larger than ourselves and we just go back to that. We're connected in some way that I don't understand and you don't understand. But this is the best way I can explain it to you."

Burst your bubbles has come to be a meaningful image for me when faced with troubled times. When life seems constricting or I can't find a way out of an unpleasant predicament, it's helpful to remember that I may merely be trapped inside the bubble of my own ego, critically limiting my vision and shutting off hidden resources. A key to making useful magic in our lives is knowing how to burst our bubbles and reconnect with the sea of creative energy all around us—without actually having to die, of course!

STEP INTO THE NEXT WORLD

The shaman keeps a foot in both worlds because he has access to the unlimited, eternal world of spiritual insight and creativity while still operating in the everyday, mundane world of physical limits and social constraints. So I suspect that when Eduardo finally burst the bubble of his physical existence, he simply stepped with both feet into a world that was already familiar from his visits there as a practicing shaman.

Make Your Own Adventures

1. UNDERTAKE A VISION QUEST

Two decades ago, the "vision quest" was still an arcane ritual common to many indigenous cultures but unknown to most modern Westerners, save for a few quirky anthropologists. Today it's rapidly becoming one of the hottest tools for reinvigorating the corporate soul. If you don't believe me, listen to this report from *Business Week* in late 1999:

> For the past six years, 300 Xerox employees . . . have participated in "vision quests" as part of the struggling copier

company's $400 million project to revolutionize product development. Alone for 24 hours with nothing more than sleeping bags and water jugs in New Mexico's desert or New York's Catskill Mountains, the workers have communed with nature, seeking inspiration and guidance about building Xerox's first digital copier-fax-printer. . . .

One epiphany came when a dozen engineers in northern New Mexico saw a lone, fading Xerox paper carton bobbing in a swamp of old motor oil at the bottom of a pit. They vowed to build a machine that would never end up polluting another dump. . . . The eventual result: the design and production of Xerox's hottest seller, the 265DC, a 97%-recyclable machine. Word of the program's success spurred senior executives from companies as diverse as Ford, Nike, and Harley-Davidson to make pilgrimages to Rochester to get a firsthand look.

Ready to give it a try now?

> *Conduct your own vision quest. Take a vigorous half-day hike into some familiar woods. Eat lightly or not at all. As you hike, concentrate on an important question or challenge that you've been facing lately. Be aware that you are giving the question to the spirits within nature, no longer trying to figure it out yourself. When you get tired and hungry, pick up a fist-sized rock and stare at it until you see an answer to your question.*

Yes, you read that right. A traditional Native American practice called rock-seeing is an excellent beginner's exercise for acquiring shamanic vision. This miniquest will introduce you to the fundamental elements of shamanic work: asking a question of spirit, or the "other side"; putting the body and mind under some stress in order to induce an altered state of consciousness; and finally, retrieving a vision from nature itself.

In rock-seeing, the meaningless textures and patterns of a random stone eventually arrange themselves into some kind of meaningful map, or symbolic image, that will answer any question you have posed in a most surprising way. As you gain practice, you can make your vision quests longer and more adventurous or join a group quest. But the ultimate aim is not to stage the most arduous quest in order to get the "biggest" vision. The aim is developing the knack of gaining useful insights and inspiration from the other side whenever you need them. That's how visionaries get their illuminating reputation!

2. CONSULT THE ORACLE

If a glitch in your personal Way-back Machine keeps you from time-traveling to ancient Greece in search of oracles, then it may be useful to find a more accessible portal to life's great answers. For those moments when no Himalayan guru awaits on our doorstep and even late-night psychic hot lines seem unreliable, it is good to know that there is the wisest of sages closer than our phone: our own subconscious. And a time-honored hot line to your own hidden wisdom can be dialed up with a few coins and a venerable handbook.

> *Consult the oracles of synchronicity for new insights into the most vexing or profound challenges of your life.*

The most accessible and time-honored volume of oracular advice is the *I Ching*, the ancient Chinese Book of Changes. In the foreword to an early translation, the Swiss psychologist Carl Jung described the often startling prognostic properties of the book as an example of *synchronicity*. He explains: "Synchronicity takes the coincidence of events in space and time as meaning something more than mere chance, namely a peculiar interdependence of objective events . . . among themselves as well as with the subjective states of the observer or observers."

While the ancient Chinese attributed the accuracy of the *I Ching* to "spiritual agencies acting in mysterious ways," Jung's explanation is somewhat more down to earth. If a handful of matches is thrown to the floor, he explains, they form a pattern characteristic of that moment—a symbolic map of present reality. If you know how to read that unique map, it's possible to draw from this simple pile of matches some very useful insights about your place in the current scheme of reality. Fortune-tellers of all types, from tea-leaf readers to sidewalk Tarot card interpreters, profess to being able to decipher such patterns.

Although I am a skeptic about most things esoteric, it seems to me that the people who organized the system of trigrams and hexagrams that comprises the *I Ching* three thousand years ago had some kind of inside track on the deep nature of things. At least three Asian physicists credit the *I Ching* with helping them win Nobel prizes in particle physics; in his book *Powers of the Mind*, Adam Smith claimed it could predict stock market movements. Like consulting a wise old friend, I seldom make a major move in my life without asking for a piece of advice from the *I Ching*. More often than not, it is accurate enough for my jaw to drop and my head to shake in incredulity.

A number of popular interpretations of this oracle are now available in books and on the Internet; two of the most respected editions are translated by Richard Wilhelm and R. L. Wing. Beyond the book, you'll need only three coins about the size of a quarter. Many people like to use the classic Chinese coins designed for use with the *I Ching*, but in fact any kind of coin with heads and tails will do. Follow the instructions provided in the book to learn how to cast the oracle.

Although the *I Ching* may be the best example of systemized synchronicity, don't overlook commonplace oracles available to the open mind at every turn. Just take your subconscious out of park as you back out of your driveway and see where it steers you. Pose a problem, like a current impasse at work or a difficult relationship, and notice the information coming your way seemingly at random. How does the giant image of a mountain biker on a billboard staring at you across three lanes of traffic make you feel? Time to hit the open road or head for higher ground? Or, instead, do you feel like it's time to change gears, slow down, catch your breath, and give those overpumped muscles a break?

Only you can know. A flick of the radio dial, too, may bring lyrical insights about an impending decision. Bumper stickers, my favorite freeway omen, require more decoding, but you never know when you'll chance across the wisdom that counts for you in the moment: Character Counts; If You Think Education Is Expensive, Try Ignorance; or Visualize Whirled Peas.

3. SHAMANIZE YOUR OFFICE

Since we spend the majority of life's waking hours at work, the workplace is where we most need to feel the magic of life. Too often, people bring only a minuscule amount of their potential with them to work and then wonder why their work lives are so dull and unsatisfactory. Likewise, employers invite only fragments of their new employee's personality through the front door each day, then wonder why they aren't getting all they had hoped for from their new hire. Across the board, today's most profitable organizations are those whose environment and culture support ongoing employee interest in the mission, the process, and each other.

> *Make life more interesting in the workplace by drawing up a list of three concrete things you can do to create a more interesting and provocative professional environment. Try them one by one until you've "shamanized" your office with a magical energy that wasn't there before. Don't be afraid to fail or look foolish.*

Need suggestions? Here are three ideas drawn from my own consulting experience. Use them as is, or for inspiration to come up with new ideas of your own.

- Reshape the energies of your office. Can't afford a feng shui specialist? Not to worry—it doesn't take a mystic to rearrange the furniture and see if your mood or productivity improves when the ficus plant is there instead of there. But instead of moving things at random, try a shamanic approach to redirecting the flow of energy in your office: Take a seat in the middle of the room and visualize your immediate environment in detail. Holding the mental picture of your office in your mind, silently thank each major feature of the room (your chair, desk, computer screen, plants, and so on) for serving you faithfully. Then ask each of the helpers you've identified where it would like to move, if anywhere, to optimize your productivity and bring the greatest possible happiness into the room. You may be surprised to hear what your inanimate yet loyal "co-workers" have to say! A shaman recognizes the life force inherent in every little thing—and learning to tune in to their subtle energies is what gives the shamanic practitioner seemingly magical powers.

- Bring the Buddha to work. Or the Prophet, or the man from Galilee. Many people find that keeping a picture of a great spiritual teacher or visionary thinker within their field of vision helps them remember great virtues they mean to bring to their field of endeavor and focuses their concentration when the everyday forces of chaos threaten to overwhelm the mind. Most workplaces are far more open to spiritual icons than they used to be, as long as you're discreetly placing pictures or symbols for your own use and not trying to sell your religious ideas to co-workers. My favorites: Albert Schweitzer and the Dalai Lama.

- Make your own *mesa*. Most of us already instinctively create *mesas* on our physical desktops, populating them with photos of loved ones, "Far Side" or "Dilbert" calendars, and souvenirs of recent vacations. Why not invest a little deeper thought and intention to increase your desktop power?

  Start at home. Which objects held in the palm of your hand seem to give you strength? Which objects in your field of vision yield an insight or feeling of serenity? In short, what are the most potent symbols you could appropriately place in your work area to remind you of your inner life? Select a few of these objects and allow them to find their appropriate places within, or close to, your immediate workspace. At different times, my *mesa* has consisted of a bullet casing and a small woven cross given to me by the mothers of the disappeared in El Salvador; a lighter from a Patagonian gaucho; a clay figurine from Eduardo; and photos of my family.

  The next step requires only that you take a moment to supply what Eduardo called "the juice." Allow enough time to hold each object and consider its importance in your life. Ask to embody the wisdom, strength, or commitment to a cause or meaning it symbolizes. Do this before placing each object on your *mesa* and repeat the dedication at especially stressful or discouraging moments at work. Taking a moment to tune in to the higher truths and energies represented by your power objects is not an escape from reality. Indeed, it's a simple but effective means to restore your soul and return to the tasks at hand inspired, revitalized, and ready to participate more fully than ever.

Keep on Your Bearing

In the end, that is the real work of the explorer:

to share all that you have learned,

to make it available to others, and to

close the cycle that you started

when you began the journey.

—Robert Ballard

The gaucho "El Loco" Rivera

CHAPTER 9

Going Loco with the Gaucho Guru

Although my time with Eduardo Calderón had given me some valuable insights, I wasn't ready at that point to make use of them. There was a dull ache in my soul; I knew that there was still a corner for me to turn in my personal quest, I just didn't know what it was. So I kept on walking.

Tape recorder in hand, I headed off on a yearlong project to collect data for a doctoral dissertation. My bright idea was to find out what made life worth living for the mountain folk of the Andes. My methodology was simplicity itself: I would merely ask "What is the meaning of life?" and the hardy natives would provide me with precious nuggets of indigenous wisdom. Unfortunately I was not prepared for a small complication: no one there would have the slightest idea of what I was talking about.

"The most important thing in life?" Isolina de Riquelme wondered aloud, wiping her weathered hands on a soiled apron. Her brow was furrowed, but her deep brown eyes shone like a small girl's. There was a moment of pained silence as she glanced at

José, her husband, for help. Hospitality demanded they answer the strange question of a vagabond gringo who had arrived at their cabin home in the mountains of Chile. Still, these questions were hard to understand.

"Yes," I repeated, "in your life, what do you value most? What is the most important thing?"

"Important . . . ," reflected Isolina. Finally, her eyes brightened as the answer came to her. "Small animals. Yes, it would have to be small animals!" Now she seemed to feel confident. "Chickens especially." She turned to her husband, then they both grinned victoriously.

Work Is Life

During three months of travel in the mountains of Chile, I met many families like that of Isolina and José Riquelme. They were all Mapuches, or Araucanas, descendants of an ancient tribe that avoided the conquering Spaniards by moving high into the mountains. There, oxcarts still bounce along on narrow trails, and all necessary tools are made on backyard forges. The homes of these hardy natives are called *rucas*—drafty, two-room log shelters with dirt floors. One room is for sleeping, the other is organized around the hole in the floor that serves as both oven and stove. A cook pot hangs from links of chain suspended from a wooden roof beam; cooking temperatures are managed with different lengths of chain, while bread is baked directly in the ashes. The native decor depends heavily on soot and burlap, inducing a powerful sense of time travel. Often there is not a single household accoutrement in these *rucas* that would distinguish this century from the previous one—or the one before that, for that matter.

I was the first backpack-bearing outsider to travel these rutted roads. Everywhere I received the same welcome: an initial suspicion followed by kindness and generosity, generosity made all the more poignant by the presence of such obvious poverty. Perhaps it was my Spanish, but no one could decipher my questions. If I got any answer to my meaning-of-life survey, it was always the same. "Work," said the men in their patchwork clothes, holding callused hands to warm over the fire. "Work," said the women, patching those same clothes, eyes tearing from smoke. "Work is life."

While my heart went out to such good people living very difficult lives, their routine answer made little sense to me. Work is making a living, I thought. But that hardly constituted all of life!

Nicolas Sánchez, a retired Chilean *huaso*, or cowboy, brought his family to live with him in a remote hanging valley only a few miles from the unmarked border with Argentina. A handsome man whose head of dark hair belied his claim of eighty-plus years on earth, he bore a natural dignity. His oldest daughter, Rigoberta, suggested that Nicolas inherited his bearing from his father, a Mapuche warrior chief. In the evenings, the children were entertained with my stories and harmonica playing; in the daytime, we chased their small herd of goats around the brambly hillsides and hauled firewood down from the mountain with leather ropes. One afternoon, Nicolas and family nervously faced my tape recorder. Uneasy about their first interview, they were nonetheless too gracious to refuse.

"What is your life about, Nicolas? What gives your life meaning?" I asked. The ensuing silence went on for several agonizing minutes while the family smiled awkwardly and I chuckled nervously, utterly failing to put anyone, including myself, at ease. Finally I resumed: "What has the most importance in your life? What makes life worth living?"

Nicolas stared at me with something akin to terror. I felt horribly guilty for causing my kind host such discomfort and finally clicked off the tape recorder, shrugging apologetically.

Then Nicolas motioned to his great-granddaughter, who approached him with a giggle. He scooped her up and set her on his knee. Still saying nothing, Nicolas Sánchez smiled at me.

"How do you like the horse?"

In truth, I loved it already. A good horse for sale in these parts was harder to find than an honest man; an honest man selling a good horse was nearly a miracle. Yet I seemed to have found one, and I felt I deserved it. I'd left Chile in morose disappointment, for no one there seemed to have much to say about what I considered to be life's big questions. My dissertation looked dead in the water, and even worse,

I was bored. After a couple of months, the poor yet contented gentlefolk and pastoral landscapes had begun to lose their charm. My limited attention span required a considerably more dramatic environment. Now, here in Argentine Patagonia, I was getting outfitted for true adventure.

You could tell by my outfit that I was a gaucho. After all, I'd made a stop at the local Gaucho Depot, a general store in Los Antiguos. I had my baggy *bombacha* trousers, black beret, traditional rope-soled shoes called *alpargatas,* and calfskin boots with spurs. My dagger was thrust into my faja, a wide woven belt, completing the outfit. And now I even had a horse.

"And the dog?" I asked, indicating the shaggy animal sitting beside my new steed.

"The dog . . . ," said the honest man, "goes with the horse."

And he did. The German shepherd mutt called Indio was inseparable from Barrilito, the big white horse. Like an overprotective sibling, yapping and worrying, the canine seemed to have no other interest in life than shadowing my transportation. So I had a horse, and the horse had a dog; together we made a team. I handed over the equivalent of seventy dollars for horse, tack and saddle, and dog. The next day we rode out of town. Sort of.

Just past the last house, Barrilito broke into a rough trot and I found myself bouncing up and down in the saddle. I pulled on the reins to no avail; Indio circled, yipping wildly as Barrilito shifted into a gallop. By the time I hauled him to a stop, my beret was a hundred yards behind us. After dismounting and recovering my hat, I realized I was in trouble. We were in the middle of the Argentine pampa, which means "space" in the Tehuelche Indian lingo. Looking around, I quickly discovered that there were no logs or large rocks in space. In fact, as far as I could see, there were neither objects nor geological features to provide the additional foot of height required for my legs to reach the short stirrups of my tall horse.

Gamely I grabbed the saddle and threw one leg up. Indio barked and Barrilito took a couple steps as I slipped ingloriously to the ground. I hopped on one foot and tried again with the same result: Indio barked and Barrilito obligingly trudged forward, with me dangling off his broadside. After traveling some distance in this maddening greenhorn shuffle, I got serious. Holding on with two hands I vaulted high into the air, causing Indio to howl with derision as I landed in a belly flop, fully extended across the top of the horse. My spurs raked Barrilito's back haunches and we shot off at top speed across the plains. Paralyzed by the speed gained by the great animal's pounding hooves, I held on for dear life, reins in one hand, a fistful of Barrilito's mane in the other. Indio was hugely entertained, racing with us like the wind, barking madly at the clumsiest horseman he had surely ever seen. Thus we headed south.

So I wasn't a real gaucho yet—not by a long shot. The archetypal Argentine gaucho is a legendary horseman of fiery disposition with a predilection for moonlit travel down lonely trails. Fanatical about freedom, the gaucho is a man of action whose actions are nobody's business but his own. An intriguing virtue of the gaucho is the ability to battle with clever words in the form of a song or riddle, but to draw knives and resolve matters in a fair fight is no sin. Because of his propensity to right wrongs on the spot without delay, a true gaucho has likely spent some time in flight from the law. That's why he does not ask a fellow traveler's name; he simply offers him his hospitality.

The term gaucho is an honorific. In Argentina today, a *gauchada* is a kind favor. And *la gauchesca* has come to mean a natural nobility, a rough but genuine elegance of spirit. The word *caballero*, literally the man on horseback, means "gentleman" and also describes the gaucho. He lives in no city, has no house or fixed address; his home is the back of his horse. Chivalrous, a word deriving from "horse," also befits the gaucho. Though he may drink prolifically and swear often, he is a man of honor above all else. He is *servicial*, of service to others, and he must be self-effacing. In fact, any man who would refer to himself as a gaucho is not fit to be one. The term must be used only in bestowing an honor upon another.

I am not the first gringo to admire the style of the gaucho. In 1833, Charles Darwin, naturalist aboard the HMS *Beagle*, noted, "The gauchos or country people are very superior to those who reside in towns. The gaucho is invariably most obliging, polite and hospitable. I have not met one instance of rudeness or inhospitality." He also noted their penchant for knife fighting, which often resulted in bloodshed.

The word "gaucho" derives from the Tehuelche Indian *huacho*, a word equivalent to "maverick," meaning an orphaned or undomesticated animal. "Wild and woolly" aptly describes the gauchos, for they have always been wild; in past centuries they carved out their lives in the no-man's-land between European and Indian societies. Today, those few who are left are mostly woolly, making their living as hired hands on sheep estancias in the wildest regions of the country. With troops of horses and the attendant dogs, gauchos still roam the remote corners of the Argentine west, much as cowboys once did the American frontier, finding a few weeks of work here and there before moving on.

On my climbing trips, I had seen these rough-hewn characters in the bars of Patagonia. I'd heard them strum guitars and sing their plaintive milongas and sambas about lost love, trusty horses, and wine. I was convinced that if anyone knew the secret of life's meaning, it would be some old gaucho guru who had taken his horse and wisdom in hand and entered the wilderness, leaving the ordinary world far behind. I wanted to be among these Latin cowboys when they passed the gourd filled with bitter *yerba maté* around the campfire circle and to know what they seemed to know.

While I daydreamed about growing into my outfit, my horse and my dog spirited me across an otherworldly landscape. Hundreds of miles of featureless Patagonian flats gave way to green-blue turrets and towers, a seemingly extraterrestrial scenery comprised of crumbling shale. Condors wheeled effortlessly overhead on ten-foot wingspans, waiting for something to die, eyeing me hopefully. Llamalike guanaco huddled in packs and stared at me with dark, curious eyes before abruptly scattering up the rocky slopes, disappearing into the mists descending from the mountain glaciers. I heard the shrieks of foxes, followed tracks of mountain lions, and galloped through flocks of flamingos standing stock-still in the gray lagoons. It was a wild and beautiful ride indeed.

And then there was the wind. On the days we rode with the wind at our backs, I thought about how two sets of roller skates strapped to Barrilito's hooves would allow us to sail effortlessly all day. When we turned to face the wind, it seemed we had to gallop all day just to keep from losing ground. Each night I tied Barrilito to the strongest bush I could find. I knew he wouldn't run off because there was nowhere for him to go; I just didn't want him to blow away.

Every few days we came upon a *puesto*, a shepherd's shack, usually a lean-to of adobe with a sheet metal roof that whipped and snapped in the wind. The inside offered little shelter; accustomed to falling sideways, the rain entered as it pleased. It would turn the dirt floor to mud and wet the cow skulls and sheepskins that were often the sole furnishings. If the *puestero* himself happened to be in, there was always a warm welcome accompanied by a chunk of mutton in a watery stew, some fried bread, and *yerba maté*. If nothing else, there was *yerba maté*.

Yerba maté makes you holler hi-de-ho. A relative of the holly, the active ingredient of this herb is mateine, a close cousin of caffeine. The dried and powdered leaves are placed into a hollow gourd, then a pot of near-boiling water is poured, always backhand, into the leaves. A metal straw is inserted with a twist. From mouth to mouth goes the maté, the host refilling the container after each guest sucks it dry. Tiredness subsides and conversation grows more animated as the herb takes effect. "Gracias," says a guest, at last, indicating he is through. "Provecho," responds the host. Not until all have said *gracias* and received a *provecho* in turn is the ritual over.

My hosts were always gracious. A human presence in a landscape so vast and inhospitable is a jewel too rare to squander. Still, they were not the gauchos of folklore but simple *puesteros*, shepherds tending to the flocks of the wealthy, landholding patrons. Often the shepherds were of the same race of people I had met on the other side of the mountains and many miles north, Chileans from the island of Chiloé and the hills around Temuco who had come to Argentina in search of work. Secure in their huts, no more than a day's ride from a roadhead, they always expressed amazement at meeting someone on horseback traveling across the pampas, living in the wilds.

"People don't do that anymore. No one lives in the woods. No one but a madman like Loco Rivera," said a *puestero* whose cabin I stumbled upon one day.

"Loco Rivera?" I puzzled. Crazy Rivera?

"El Loco Rivera, the hermit who lives in tree stumps and eats his own horses. He is crazy. All the other real gauchos died a long time ago."

I had to meet him.

We averaged about twenty miles a day, traveling from first light to last. Some days I almost felt like I knew what I was doing, sipping maté in the morning calm, a faithful dog curled at my feet while my big white horse grazed peacefully. With the affection born of shared adversity, both horse and dog had accepted me into their circle.

There were some good days when I successfully followed rock cairns up and over mountains, then downward through the knee-high bunch grass toward the golden purple plains below, the leather of my saddle creaking agreeably beneath me. On other days, my sleeves kept unrolling and my butt blistered from the endless hours of pounding against hard leather. My spurs caught in my stirrups, my baggy pants kept coming out of my boots.

Then one day my saddlebags came loose. Pots and pans, leather ropes, and camera gear scattered across the landscape. No sooner did I recover from that debacle than my cinch came undone. Still in the saddle, I rolled under my horse's belly. This was too much for even the good-natured Barrilito; he reared up, bucking and whinnying in fright. I kicked free and tumbled headfirst to the ground. Indio licked my face in consolation.

At an outpost near a windswept lake, I was able to convince the shepherd, Alfredo Gomez, to sell me a horse to carry my gear. The horse was suspiciously nameless and hard to lasso, but he was another *tordillo*, the same gray-white coloration and size as Barrilito. Real gauchos prefer matching horses.

"He's a little wild," warned my host as I handed him four million pesos, the equivalent of sixty dollars. I named the horse Alfredo, in honor of his previous owner. Our travel party now numbered four.

A few days later, I met René and Herminio Avilez along the windswept shores of Lake Pueyrredón. It had been a long day and I was very tired. Taking them up on their offer of a roof for the night, I followed them up a narrow canyon trail above a racing river to their ranch. Constructed over a century ago, Estancia El Gaucho must once have been quite impressive. When I arrived it was not much more than a ruin of splintered beams and cracked plaster. Dressed in full gaucho regalia—belts studded with silver coins, big hats with upturned brims—the Avilez brothers themselves seemed to have stepped out of a living history museum.

"Being way up here in these canyons, I guess you don't get a lot of foreign visitors," I said lightly as I accepted the steaming maté gourd.

"Well, not often," replied Herminio, the older brother, reflecting on my comment quite seriously. "But there were those other Americans . . ."

I felt disappointed; apparently I had not wandered as far as I thought.

"Sí, los bandidos americanos," recalled René. The American bandits. "It is a story our grandfather would tell. Americans, three of them, two men and a woman. They came and stayed for a month. Yes, those gringos became good friends with my grandfather. He told us that the woman could take a pistol and put her initials in a tree—one shot after another—at fifteen meters. That tree right out the window, there. Bark is grown over now." He rose and threw more wood into the stove.

"What happened to them?" I asked.

"Oh, they had to leave suddenly. One morning they just

saddled up, rode into the canyon, and crossed the glaciers into Chile. Horses and all. No one's ever done that before or since. Grandpa used to laugh at how a whole regiment of police showed up that same day. Turned out that these Americans had been robbing banks all the way from Bolivia to Río Gallegos."

I collapsed in laughter. I, too, had heard stories of the gang that pulled a few jobs in these parts. Now I had the satisfaction of knowing I was the first gringo to warm himself in that kitchen since Butch, the Sundance Kid, and Etta Place.

Crossing the Río Roble, everything seemed to fly apart. Alfredo went crazy, bucking and leaping and sending my gear sailing with the wind. Bee sting? Saddle burr? Packhorse dementia? Later we traversed a meadow along the shores of Lake Burmeister, which abruptly transformed into a swamp. Both horses sank to their bellies in the quagmire. Lurching free, Alfredo snapped his rawhide tether and made for the woods. It took a couple of hours for Barrilito, Indio, and me to corral him in a box canyon.

That was enough excitement for one day, so I made camp right there in the lee of a sheltering grove of linga trees. No sooner did I sit down than I heard Indio's warning bark; Alfredo had slipped his hobbles and headed for the hills once more. There was another hour's chase in mud and muck before we could capture and lead him home.

Sitting by the fire, I cursed Alfredo for causing so much trouble even as I admired his renegade desire for freedom. I thought that I could offer him a little heartfelt advice from my own experience: Freedom does not equal happiness, my friend. Look at me. If anyone had ever been free, it was I. So why was I not feeling joyous and carefree? Too often, it seemed there were two people living my life. One came up with colorful, romantic schemes, the other had to live them. One sold can't-miss real estate opportunities to the other guy, the sucker, who ended up floundering in the swampland. Freedom is the itch that can't be scratched, I silently told Alfredo. What was I after, anyway?

Too tired to think any more cheery thoughts, I decided it was a great time to take photographs. I positioned the camera on a nearby stone to capture myself sitting by the fire, sucking my maté, attempting to look far more contented and masterful than I felt. The tiny red light blinked and I struck my pose just as a gust of wind arrived, knocking my camera from the rock with a crash. I rushed over, reset the camera, resumed my pose. The wind laughed and made a fool of me again. I cursed as I went to reposition the camera once more.

"Thank God the ground was there," a voice boomed from nowhere.

"Huh?" I looked up, startled. Above me, not ten yards away, stood a chestnut stallion. Perched atop the horse was an impressive rider, the handle of a large knife protruding prominently from his sash. A beret and bushy blond beard framed eyes that gleamed a strangely luminous blue.

"I said thank God the ground was there," he repeated, stone-faced. "Now it can't fall any farther." His sharp eyes bore right through me.

"Hmm. Yes, thank God for the ground," I muttered, recognizing the gaucho's verbal challenge and scrambling for a rejoinder. "Yes . . . if it weren't for the ground we'd have to string wire from the trees and hang the cows from large hooks just so they could graze."

"Ha!" snorted the man on horseback, his face lightening. "Muy bien, compañero." With strong hands he yanked the rope to his snorting packhorse as his dogs circled closer to sniff me. Below the cowboy's long coat, bare knees protruded from torn bombacha trousers tucked into rubber boots. Studying me, he rolled a cigarette and lit it on the first try, undeterred by the wind.

"You are not from here, *compañero*. You are not one of those *guardaparques*, eh? One who tells you not to make a fire here? Not to sleep there? You have not come here to tell me where I can breathe and where I can shit?"

"No, señor, I believe it is your right to shit anywhere you please."

"Bueno, así es." The stranger nodded his head with great seriousness; I seemed to be scoring some points. "You are alone, *compañero?* Traveling with no one but these horses and a dog?"

"Sí."

"Muy bien. That is unusual." He flicked away the cigarette. "Tomorrow you will follow my tracks. Just stay on my tracks, and you and your horses will stop falling into the swamp." He arched his eyebrows to confirm that he had been observing the day's entertainment. "Stay on the trail through the trees and in a few hours you will come to my *puesto*. There you can spend the night."

Pulling his reins to one side, he flicked his horse's flanks with his leather whip. The stallion turned with a snort. "Remember, the only way to cross this swamp is to follow my tracks," he called over his shoulder.

"What is your name?" I yelled back, curiosity overtaking my manners.

"My name?" laughed the stranger with the wild eyes. "They call me Rivera."

El Loco Rivera, I murmured to the wind.

The next day, following Rivera's tracks, I crossed the swamp. As if walking on water, we skimmed over the surface in a miraculous ten-minute passage through the same topography that had us floundering for hours the day before. Rivera knew where the secure stones were; had he put them there? Was this how he kept the park rangers at bay?

The day was calm; even Alfredo behaved himself. We covered a dozen miles in a matter of hours without encountering a head-wind, allowing us more miles to the gallop. Finally, a wooded trail led us uphill to an old corral visible in a clearing. Smoke rose from a three-sided shanty. Tying the horses, I stepped around the corner to the open side of the building.

Rivera sat on a bleached cow skull, warming his outstretched hands over an open fire. His interior decorating scheme was an eclectic mix of Swiss Family Robinson and *The Silence of the Lambs:* scattered bones of assorted sizes, blackened pots, rusted cans, animal skins. His bed consisted of a few logs piled with cowhides. Rising to his feet with a half bow and sweep of an arm, he announced, "Welcome to Casa Rivera. Please, *caballero*, have a seat." He motioned elegantly to a second cow skull as if it were a throne. "Shall we have some *yerba?*"

For a couple of minutes the only noise was the occasional snort of the horses, the crackle of the fire. Pinholes of light in the sheet metal of the shack's roof illuminated the rising smoke in tiny beams. Rivera packed the gourd, poured the water, took the customary first water—bitter and leafy—in his mouth and spat it out before handing me the gourd.

Since he was too gaucho to inquire openly, I explained that I was from the States, traveling along the mountains of Patagonia, learning about the old ways and investigating what was most important to people there.

"You have come to find the meaning of life," he declared.

Startled to hear this rustic character speaking my dissertation theme, I stuttered in agreement. "*Sí!* That's it! Exactly! *Sí, señor.*"

"You have come to the right place. I have thought much about the subject and after many years have discovered the answer." Suddenly dramatic, Rivera took the gourd and sucked loudly.

I scrunched closer to gather the wisdom of my host, cursing the fact that my tape recorder was packed away in my saddlebags.

This was too good to be true. Rivera cleared his throat in preparation for his pronouncement. "The most important thing in life is this . . . you must always be *mugriento*."

"*Mugriento?*" I asked, certain I have heard not correctly. As far as I knew, *mugriento* meant filthy, grimy, or greasy.

"*Mugriento,*" he affirmed. "Absolutely."

I eyed my host warily.

"Look at me, for example, I am so *mugriento* that I never have to worry about getting wet. Water runs right off me. It makes me so proud that when I walk down the street I can hold my head high." Rivera lifted his chin, assuming a regal pose. "I hear the people say, 'Now look at that fellow. He is *mugriento!*'"

Even if Rivera was putting me on, I couldn't deny that he walked his talk. His clothes were soiled rags, his socks nothing more than burlap bags wrapped around his feet. There was a landfill under his nails. And a sweaty pungency rose from him that was, to say the least, unforgettable. A smile playing on the corners of his mouth made me uncertain of exactly how to go along with this gaucho's verbal game.

"Yes, but being so *mugriento,*" I ventured, "it must be difficult to have many friends."

"Ah, but I have a very good friend."

"Who is that?" I asked.

"You, *compañero*. I think you and I are going to be very good friends."

"But you must have other friends?" I blurted without thinking, taken aback by my host's sudden familiarity.

"Sí," he smiled, "there is also Sparky."

"Sparky is your friend?"

"Sparky is my friend, yes. Also my skunk."

"Your skunk?" I exclaimed. "You have a skunk for a friend? Where does he live?"

"Under my bed."

"Isn't there a terrible smell?"

"There is," admitted Rivera. "But you know, I think he is getting used to it."

Not being equipped with my own air freshener like Sparky, I pitched my tent twenty feet from Rivera's shack. When I awoke late the next morning, Rivera had prepared an amazingly tasty porridge of oats and raisins. For lunch he fried bread in hot fat; we wolfed that down with cold mutton and cheese. For dinner there was a meat stew with potatoes and rice. Rivera was a gracious host and a surprisingly good cook, so when he invited me to stay another day, I agreed. Soon a couple more days passed, and we had done little more than swap stories, drink *yerba maté*, and eat. Although it appeared that we were accomplishing nothing, Rivera explained that we were practicing one of life's great virtues, *flojera*. Laziness.

When I asked him what his job description was here at the *puesto*, he rose slowly from his skull stool and peered out the door at some cows. "I watch the animals. Yes, there they are." He settled back down on his seat. "That was work!" he declared. "At least now we can relax. We are done for the day!"

Gazing out the door one afternoon, Rivera mused, "You know, I had a fellow once ask me why I don't get a real job. Do some real work, he said. When I asked him why I should work he said, 'You could earn money.' I asked him what would I want with money? He said, 'Put it in the bank.' Now what good is money in a bank? He tells me, 'It builds and builds until after many years you have so much money that you can stop working. You can just sit around and enjoy life!'" Rivera shook his head. "I told him that's what I am doing right now."

I stayed with Rivera for days, doing little but talking, eating, and drinking *yerba maté*. Despite his dedication to inactivity, Rivera was never too lazy to keep my *yerba maté* gourd full. Like some odiferous, woolly mother, he hovered over my little caravan, roping a cow to come up with fresh milk and delivering oats to Alfredo and Barrilito each morning.

Finally I could abide by Rivera's schedule no longer; the search had to go on. There were more places to go and meaningful interviews to conduct. The highest passes of my trip lay ahead; that would be some real work after days of concentrated resting. As I busied myself with departure preparations, Rivera sauntered over to help me tighten the cinches on my saddle.

"Are you off to find the meaning of life?" he asked, leaning one elbow on Barrilito's broad rump. He seemed unusually serious.

"I suppose I am."

"Well, seeing as you are my *compañero* now . . . I will tell you the truth."

"Sí?" I was willing to humor my host a final time.

"There is nowhere to go," he intoned, "and nothing to do, except to be of service." That said, he nodded and walked off. That was the sum total of our farewell.

I headed on up the valley from Rivera's *puesto*. First we left behind the trees, then even the grass as Indio barked and frolicked, sending vizcacha, the high-altitude rodents of the Andes, scurrying into their holes. Barrilito slipped to his knees repeatedly on the slick tongues of ice as we crossed the snowfields while Alfredo, recalcitrant as ever, pulled back on his rope.

At dusk the lake called Lago Bello was visible. Set in a hanging valley bordered by meadows and trees, the body of water is so remote that even Rivera said he had never been there. The drop from the ridge was too steep to ride; I led my team the long way by bushwhacking through thick forest and swamp to a campsite by a stream. Rimmed by glaciers and jagged summits, the valley felt like a lost world, charged with magic.

That night the skies opened and the rain dropped like a

waterfall. Within an hour water had soaked through the stitching of my tent, drenching my bag. During a morning break in the storm, I decided to decamp, pack the horses, and escape to a lower elevation. It was the wrong move. Not a half mile from camp we were sucked into a bog; the horses flailed in the muck while Indio howled. We were still struggling when vicious weather hit us, wet snow blasting sideways in an eighty-mile-an-hour wind. The horses were panicking; I had to unload them and lift their legs free, one at a time. Somehow we got ourselves free.

Retreating uphill toward the meager shelter of the woods by the lake, I reestablished camp with hands frozen into near useless claws. I realized that I'd be lucky to survive the night, and I knew that we must move lower as soon as the storm passed—soon, I could only pray. But a week later, we were still in the same place. I lay in my tent cursing my poor instincts, my entire body numb from the cold and wet, my food now gone.

The lush green valley had become a snow-filled bowl. The horses were having a hard time digging through deepening white powder to find food. Any wood I could find was too saturated to start a fire. I spent my days curled in a tight ball, waiting to run with the first break in the weather.

Unfortunately, Alfredo had the same idea. I heard a snap and a crackle, and by the time I had peered out from the frozen tent flap he had broken loose from his rawhide hobbles. For a second we stared at each other, then I leapt barefoot from my tent and made a desperate dive at the trailing rope, missing by inches. Alfredo crashed through the low-lying branches, reached the snow in the open meadow, and broke into a run. Snorting and whinnying, the untied Barrilito trotted behind, apparently deciding I was a losing proposition. Indio, of course, ran with his old friend.

I grabbed my jacket and pants, shoved my bare feet into

boots, and took off in pursuit. In the near whiteout of blowing snow, Indio's frantic barking was my only guide. Unable to see the frozen lake, I no sooner stumbled upon it than I was in it. I hauled myself free, soaked from the waist down. Above me two pale forms trotted through a cloud across barren rock. If only I could head them off at the sheer rocks and ice wall directly above—I still had a chance.

But Alfredo was too clever. He zigzagged straight up toward the pass. Finally my legs quit; I knelt on a rock, wheezing painfully with every in-breath of the freezing air. For a moment the clouds lifted and I could see Alfredo leading the team upward, Barrilito and Indio dutifully following. "Good luck, guys," I whispered. Collecting my strength, I rose to my feet and started my way back to camp. The Grand Salz Meaning-of-Life Expedition was down to just me. Salz, party of one, chanted a voice in my head.

Carving dry tinder from the inside of an old stump, I was able to start a fire. I stayed alive by keeping a constant fire going a few feet from where I wrapped myself in my collapsed tent. By dislodging dead standing timber whose roots had rotted from moisture and dragging them over the snow into my pit, I was able to feed the flames. Holding my feet to the fire, I scorched my socks without coaxing much warmth into the flesh.

But then I discovered, to my surprise, that I felt unreasonably happy.

With the horses gone, I no longer had to worry about them running away. And no longer did I have to fear bad weather, running out of food, or getting stranded in the mountains. When you've hit bottom, nothing else can go wrong.

"Thank God the ground was there to break my fall," I muttered. "Now I can't fall any farther." Recalling the mischievous voice and penetrating blue eyes, I began to understand Rivera's clever lesson. Sometimes it takes everything going wrong to get things right in your own head.

For starters, my restless expedition in search of meaning was done. Now survival was the only goal. Days and nights passed as I sat unmoving for hours at a time, lost in a hallucinatory stream of consciousness. Sometimes I would awaken with a start, unsure of whether I'd actually been asleep, uncertain of whether I was going crazy or sane. Then I'd march around the meadow in a foot of snow, howling extemporaneous ditties to the hills.

At least no one was watching; I could laugh and sing my way into oblivion. By the fire I clutched a book of Eastern philosophy in which the author suggested that even the most heroic search might be no more than an escape from the mundane yet profound realities of ordinary life. In endless motion, said the guru, we begin to live an illusion of life instead of life itself. We become hooked on the speed of our own lives.

Now that I was stopped nearly dead in my tracks, the meaning of life was very clear: Chickens. Small animals. Loving your children. Work. Filth and laziness . . . The meaning of life is simply the appreciation of every moment of life itself.

Now I was sobbing. To my surprise, the source of my sorrow was not that I might die there—a possibility I had faced many times before—but that I might not live to do my work, to tell my tales. I swore that if I somehow survived this trip, I would live differently. I would not waste another day in busy, ceaseless seeking, searching everywhere for what was right under my own nose. Now that I knew that meaning began in one's own heart— that it was a way of seeing everything with love, rather than just trying to see everything—it was a shame that I might not be around long enough to pass on the message. To be of service.

As the naturalist John Muir said, "Sometimes God has to nearly kill us to teach us a lesson." Sometime during that long night by the fire, I managed to sleep.

In the morning, great blue gaps began to appear in the clouds above. The air was warming as snow fell in great clumps from the tree boughs above me. The sun's first rays brightened the white hillsides with gold and I could see, at last, that I would survive. I strapped my sleeping bag to my back and, with feet too swollen to wear boots, lashed flimsy slippers to my feet. Leaving everything else behind, I retraced my route through knee-deep snow over the mountains from which I had come.

Atop the first pass, I walked out of the cloud and into a blinding sunlight. Cerro Lorenzo rose huge and white against the blue sky to the west. Highest and least visited of all Patagonian summits, its abrupt appearance seemed like an omen, a blessing, a reminder not to forget the lessons of the last few days. I had to remember that there was really nowhere to go; merely being alive meant I had already arrived at my destination. As an exercise, I walked a small circle to keep from forgetting that life itself was the goal of the heroic journey. Later, knee-deep in an icy stream, I did a song and dance. If anyone had seen me, they would have thought me as loco as Rivera, dancing and walking circles when survival should have been top priority. But how was it that I felt saner than ever before?

At dusk in wet clothes and without shelter, I was not yet out of the woods, as they say. I heard a call; in the distance a lone horseman emerged from the edge of the forest. Rivera. "Compañero!" he called.

"Com . . . pa . . . ñero," I stammered as he approached, staring in amazement. "How did you know . . . ?"

"Well, your horses went by about three days ago." Rivera dismounted. "You have walked a long way. Now you will ride my horse."

"No. I can walk. It is your horse. Besides, a gaucho does not walk."

"That is why you must ride. I can only imagine where you

have been, but only a true gaucho could survive this country." There was a proud glow in his eyes. "You, my friend, are a gaucho now." Though I was too tired to acknowledge the remark, its significance was not lost on me. To this day I consider it the greatest compliment I have ever received.

Rivera dismounted, then helped me to the saddle, placing my frozen feet into the stirrups. Slowly we began our way down the valley, walking in silence in the lengthening shadows. Rivera, striding along in his black rubber boots, led the way.

"By the way, *compañero*, just curious . . . where did you go?" he asked.

"Nowhere."

"I see. And just what did you do?"

"Nothing."

"So, amigo, the meaning of life you have been looking for is—"

"Is to be of service, right?" I laughed.

"Así es, compañero," he confirmed. "But right now let's head home for some *yerba maté*. Have I ever told you about this skunk of mine?"

I asked him to tell me again.

CHAPTER 10

The Secrets of Service

My friend Jim Zuberbuhler spends his nights jumping from helicopters in the dark, hauling lost climbers off the mountain above our home.

In a typical rescue, the climber has gone missing earlier in the day; the rescue team generally doesn't get the call until about ten in the evening. Jim loads up his Toyota with the usual: ascending rings, ropes, belay devices. Soon he is leaping from a helicopter into a whiteout near the summit of Mount San Jacinto. As he tromps through knee-deep snow alone in the darkness, he may find himself wondering if he might be the next guy in need of rescuing. Perhaps by two in the morning, Jim or another rescuer finds the lost climber, a victim of mild hypothermia but usually fine otherwise. Just before dawn, Jim walks the five miles down the mountain, following the bouncing beam of his flashlight as fast as his weary legs will carry him. After all, it is a workday; he has a meeting at eight in the morning.

Even without his mountain rescue activities, Jim Zuberbuhler is one of the most caring, service-oriented people I know. He's the guy I send for when I'm sitting in my truck stuck in a snowdrift. As the founding director of Out There, an adventure outfit that mixes education with expeditions, he regularly crams forty-eight hours of enterprises into a twenty-four-hour day: fundraising for worthy causes, writing grants, traveling around developing innovative educational events. A recent Zuberbuhler effort hooked up gang kids with members of the Los Angeles Police Department for two days in the wilderness.

He is also on call, day and night, as a volunteer member of the Riverside Mountain Rescue Unit. This involvement stretches his already maximized calendar and tends to thrust him into life-threatening predicaments. After all, people don't need as much rescuing on sunny days.

Adventure + Service = Clarity

Why does Jim take time away from an already busy life and an exciting career for volunteer service? "It's about moments of clarity," he says. "On a Monday morning, I can be at my desk, perhaps a few hours after stepping out of a helicopter following a successful rescue mission, and I will feel this wonderfully clear moment. It comes from having been placed in a situation where the rules are very different and where I'm required to push past my normal physical, emotional, and even spiritual boundaries."

Jim's "moment of clarity" begins in the thick of the action itself:

> When you are dangling from the copter deck at the end of a 300-foot rope on a rock face at 2 A.M., and it's 25 degrees with a forty-mile-per-hour wind in your face, you might think that you'd be asking, "Why am I doing this when I could be safely home in bed?" But you don't think about that because you have to be completely focused on helping a

hypothermic rock climber who has broken her leg and needs immediate medical attention. You trust your fellow team members with your life and disregard your frozen hands and aching muscles. The thoughts and worries that normally clutter our lives are just not there. It is a wonderfully pure and focused experience. And rescuing others takes me places I never would go just for myself.

Jim chuckles when I call him a hero, for he sees nothing self-sacrificing in his efforts. It is just a part of what he does to make a difference in his own life. How is it that we may suspend our strong instincts to preserve personal well-being and comfort for the benefit of another? Joseph Campbell, citing Schopenhauer's essay "The Foundation of Morality," described such behavior as "an embodiment of the recognition of the metaphysical aware-ness that we are one. That our separateness is only an effect of time and space. That our true reality is unity."

We respect the hero because we recognize that he or she is an individual who has realized, and is living, this highest truth. By applauding the hero we are essentially celebrating a higher con-sciousness that can inspire us all to act more generously of our own free will.

Why would any of us choose to be heroic? To paraphrase Zuberbuhler, doing things for others takes us places we never would go just for ourselves. In service we find ourselves trans-ported to new territories—not just physically but also mentally, emotionally, and spiritually.

Dare to Care

We gain tremendous vitality whenever we choose caring as the star by which to set our sail to these new territories. Historically, it is not self-aggrandizement but altruism that has inspired heroic individuals to go the extra mile, push beyond the wall, extend the bounds of human possibility. Even more than being cared about, caring for others gives us the capacity to survive and flourish in the face of daunting circumstances that may defeat those who are struggling only to defend self-interest.

I recall an interview with a Holocaust survivor who shared a concentration camp cell block with Otto Frank, father of Anne Frank. After being informed that his entire family had been taken to another part of the camp and was most likely dead, Otto Frank made a strange request. "Call me Papa," he implored.

At first his friend resisted. "I already had a father and this man was not him," he said. "Besides, we were so close in age the idea seemed ridiculous."

"I must be someone's papa," Otto Frank implored him, tears streaming down his face. "I must be someone's papa in order to survive." So his friend agreed.

Otto Frank was the only member of his family to survive the war.

We can do for others what we cannot do for ourselves. Rising above our own desires endows us with strengths we could not summon otherwise, and harmonizing our personal goals with the higher aims of humanity maximizes our effectiveness.

Heroism may be the next stage in our spiritual evolution as a species. Human beings have a biological need for adventure; to be human is to perpetually push the limits of our understanding, explore frontiers, and define ourselves by our accomplishments. Climbing this chunk of rock, exploring that expanse of ocean bottom will always be a thrill. But the level of satisfaction gets ratcheted up several magnitudes when we know our labors serve a purpose larger, grander than ourselves.

Adventure is for oneself; heroism serves others. Adventure is daring; heroism is caring. And while acts of adventure transform the individual, acts of heroism transform the world.

Heed the Call

My neighbor Geoff Robinson is no soldier of fortune. He would never have imagined that an e-mail from an old friend would thrust him into a life-and-death situation where he would have to make a decision with international reverberations. A professor of Southeast Asian History at UCLA, he had been following the political situation in East Timor for fifteen years before the struggle for independence erupted in violence in 1999. When the opportunity to volunteer as a political affairs officer for the United Nations–sponsored plebiscite on independence came his way, he and his wife Lovisa agreed he had to go.

By September 4, the UN compound had been surrounded by the maelstrom of civil war for four days following the vote. As soon as it became obvious that the election had turned into a dramatic victory for the pro-democracy majority, the Indonesian-backed militias had turned violent. A local UN staffer, a fifty-year-old schoolteacher, was knifed in the back by militia members and died while collecting paper ballots. Suddenly it all went sour.

Fleeing the wrath of the rampaging militias, fifteen hundred East Timorese civilians had stormed the defenses of the UN compound and sought protection within its flimsy confines, along with four hundred UN international staffers. Unarmed, their survival rested entirely on the whims of the murderous mobs without and the dubious guardianship of the Indonesian Armed Forces, who openly conspired with the militias.

Vengeance was in the air. Many UN personnel had already been killed, and UN convoys had been raked with machine-gun fire intended to massacre everyone aboard. So far the death count had remained miraculously low. Day and night, the sound of automatic weapon fire filled the air. Angry militiamen brandished grenades with their pins removed, threatening to toss them over the fence into the compound. Inside, the people were denied access to food and water. The world watched as the situation within the cramped compound deteriorated daily. Suddenly the lives of the UN staffers were as uncertain as those of their fifteen hundred East Timorese guests.

And then Geoff Robinson received the news that put him in a dreadful predicament. Along with two friends he had to tell the assembled local leaders the awful truth: the UN was pulling out.

Throughout the summer, posters plastered all over the capital city of Dili had proclaimed in many languages "The UN Is with You" and "The UN Will Never Betray You." Now, after countless assurances to the East Timorese that they could vote their conscience and be unafraid of the outcome, the UN was doing exactly what it had said it would never do: beating a hasty retreat with only its own personnel in tow.

For the hundreds of families camped out in the makeshift communities within the walls of the compound, this decision meant only one thing: their lives would end horribly at the hands of the various anti-democracy terrorists. Geoff relayed a virtual death sentence to the refugees. It was the hardest thing he had ever had to do.

When he and the others were done, a diminutive nun in a white and gray habit stepped forward to break the silence. Under five feet tall, with nerves of steel, Sister Esmeralda had shepherded families under attack to the safety of the compound and had remained with them to ensure their safety. "First, we thank all of you for coming to help us choose our future," she said plainly. "We do not blame you for leaving us now. We are not angry with you. But we know that when you leave most of us will be killed, so you must excuse me if I go and tell the others so we may prepare." She paused and then added, "I don't say this with bitterness, but those who have done this will never sleep again."

"When she finished speaking," Geoff recalls, "we just looked at each other and said 'We cannot do this.'" They decided to go to the head of the UN delegation in East Timor and deliver a simple message: If you order us to evacuate tomorrow, there are many who will not go.

"Who and how many? I want to know," was the director's response. "Nothing would make me happier than to stay here." A petition was circulated. Ninety-five percent of the UN personnel responded that even if ordered to go, they would refuse.

"Once you started asking people what they would do, virtually everyone fell on the side of doing the right thing," Geoff reflects. "But until a certain moment we were all moving inexorably in the direction of doing the wrong thing."

What was that certain moment? Geoff points to the fearless response of a feisty nun. "Esmeralda's courage galvanized us. She was so impressive, so strong. I found myself thinking that if I ever had a clear choice in my life between doing something and doing nothing, this was it."

Leadership Rises to the Top

Where does courage begin? Geoff Robinson learned that "in times of crisis leadership does not always come from the top. In the UN compound, leadership did not come from those who had seniority, whose responsibility it was to lead. It came from the rank and file."

Within a week, what began as an act of civil disobedience sparked a chain reaction reaching around the world from the UN compound in Timor to the international headquarters in New York. Around 4 A.M. on September 14, after traversing the blackened hell of what was once the city of Dili, now illuminated only by the fires of buildings still in flames, the last of the refugees arrived at the airstrip. Nearly two thousand refugees and UN staffers erupted in cheers as they heard the thundering engines of the first Hercules C130 that would carry them all to safety in Australia.

"My firsthand experience showed that having moral courage is the only way to live," says Geoff. "My life would scarcely be worth living if I hadn't done what I did. It feels good that in a tough situation, I did the right thing." He's not the only one to think so; the insubordinate Geoff Robinson and the entire East Timor operation eventually received a letter of commendation from Kofi Annan, Secretary-General of the United Nations. Geoff is quick to add that he finds his actions are in no way remarkable. "I think that under the circumstances almost anybody would have done the same thing," he insists.

I think he's right: when push comes to shove, we will seldom disappoint ourselves. Stories of ordinary men and women rising to the occasion are far more common than the opposite. We all harbor greater stores of courage than we think. The opportunity to test our mettle and discover for ourselves the stuff of which we are made is the gift of adversity.

Stop Thinking about Yourself

The word "courage" is derived from the Latin word *cor*, or heart. By definition, if we are living courageously we are following our hearts. I might never have stumbled onto the importance of turning off my head and tuning in to my heart if my horses hadn't run off, leaving me to be rescued from a blizzard by a crazed hermit. Sometimes, we have to lose nearly everything, including our minds, to come to our senses.

My Patagonian horse trip was the turning point of my own hero's journey. As the people of the Andes tried to tell me all along, to seek "the meaning of life" is a meaningless pursuit. My life is meaningful as soon as I start paying attention to it and enlarge the scope of my search beyond self-interest.

Pamela Meyer, author of *Quantum Creativity: Nine Principles for a Life of Possibility*, draws on her years of experience in improvisational theater for her keynote addresses on creativity in business. To ward off the stage fright that can disorient even the most experienced of performers, Meyer relies on a bright pink Post-it note always placed on her notes for speaking. On the note she has written, "It's not about you."

"Your job is not to make yourself look good or impress the audience with how much you know about your topic," she says. "You're in big trouble if that is your chief concern. Your job is to be of service to the audience, the meeting planner, the client and everyone else with whom you collaborate to achieve the most rewarding experience possible. And the fact is that you will look good—no, great—when you focus on service."

These days I earn my living as a professional speaker. Like Meyer, I've learned from this work that I am far more likely to succeed when my intention rises above the desire to succeed. If I am looking forward to fulfilling an assignment, collecting my check, and catching the plane home, I will likely succeed in doing just that, and no more. The most incredible moments of my work always seem to happen when I stop thinking about my reputation or income potential. It's remarkable what happens every time I make the effort to learn about my audience and open my heart to their reality in a genuine way. No one cares how much you know until they know how much you care.

Make Others' Dreams Come True

My first phone call from Ken Dychtwald came at an opportune moment. Returning from a jaunt to Tibet, I had found my books and papers in a couple of cardboard cartons outside the door of my office. An official university letter in my department mailbox had been "returned to sender" from the post office in Lhasa; the missive informed me that I had been given the opportunity to begin the next phase of my life.

Hat in hand, I went job hunting, a real exercise in humility. I checked the want ads but was unable to find an entry reading "Anthropologist urgently needed. Reed boat and gaucho experience preferred." After a few weeks, my lucky big break arrived; I got a job bartending and waiting tables at minimum wage. I had never worked for minimum wage. I was forty years old.

One day before I went to work, the phone rang. "Hi, this is Ken Dychtwald," said a voice. If Loco Rivera represents the archetypal iconoclast who retreats from society to live by his own rules, Ken Dychtwald exemplifies the wild man who carves out his reputation in the thick of civilization. "Early in my career people considered me an individualist," says Dychtwald. "Now that I'm successful in business, I'm called an entrepreneur." President and CEO of Age Wave Inc., Ken is recognized as one of the nation's foremost authorities on the aging of America. His nine books include the best-selling *Age Wave*, and his predictions about societal change have appeared in a host of leading periodicals including *Fortune, Inc., Time, Newsweek*, and *The Wall Street Journal*. He founded Age Wave in 1986 as a consulting firm to guide Fortune 100 companies in marketing to the fifty-plus population. Eight years later, the company evolved into a business development incubator.

My cousin Herbie had sent a tape of one of my adventure presentations, which I had given at a few outdoor equipment stores, to Ken's parents back in New Jersey. Ken listened to it and thought I had potential. Within the week I was at his home, floating in his pool, swapping stories and talking ideas. Ken volunteered to send a letter to a few people, help me create a publicity strategy, and make it work. Within two months I was no longer behind the bar. Within a year I had paid back my debts and was speaking full-time.

Create a Circle of Success

Why did Ken choose to appear in my life and help turn it around? Ken stakes no claim to sainthood. He sees himself as being as self-centered as the next guy. But he recognizes the roles others have played in his success, and as a way to show his appreciation, he enjoys reaching out to help.

"No matter how hard I work and no matter how clever I think I am, almost everything that has happened for me is a result of someone choosing to help me," says Ken. "You learn to be a helper when you've been blessed with having people help you."

Ken doesn't talk much about ethical obligations or spiritual laws; his motivation is less philosophical than that. "It's fun," he reveals—so much fun, in fact, that the satisfaction he derives from mentoring other people often exceeds the pleasures of his own success.

> I have a big staff now and it's part of the reason I built the company. The conventional reason to build a company is so you can make a lot more money than you could alone. But I built my company in part so that I could have a lot of people around me whose lives I can have some fun playing a role in. I add ideas or make connections so that other people's lives begin to follow a better path. For me, that's one of life's incredible satisfactions.

For many of us, serving others may seem an impossible luxury when it seems like it is all we can do to keep up with the challenges of daily life. The more stressed we are, the less likely we are to feel that we can afford the time, attention, or compassion to help out. And when we finally accrue some hard-won vacation time, serving in a soup line or volunteering at a senior center may not sound like the kind of break we'd like to take from the rigors of work.

See the Things You Can't See

"In the last few years, I'd begun to feel that perhaps I was not giving enough because I was more focused on the bottom line, in my heart of hearts, than I really wanted to be," admits Ken. "I thought to myself, who could be a positive influence for me? The person I spotted was Jimmy Carter. Here is a former president with plenty of power and connections. Rather than spending his retirement playing golf or sitting on a board of directors, he has chosen to contribute as much of himself as is humanly possible to help those less fortunate."

Through some lucky breaks, Ken Dychtwald came to spend a morning with the former president at the Carter Center in Atlanta. Their backgrounds were pretty different: Carter, the Baptist peanut farmer from Georgia, versus Dychtwald, the Jewish kid from Newark, New Jersey. Ken also mentioned to Carter the difference in their ages; in his late forties, Ken was then roughly the age of Carter during his presidency. "What would you say is the big difference in the way you see life now compared to when you were in your forties?" Ken asked.

"When I was your age, I thought the things that mattered most in life were the things you could see," Carter responded. "Now I've come to understand that the things that really matter are the things you cannot see: friendship and love and kindness, helping other people. These are the deeper rewards in life. The more I give, the better I feel. The more I give, the more complete and happy I am."

Increase Your Energy

A few months later, Ken would get to see Carter's style of giving in action at a Habitat for Humanity project in Houston. This time he was not alone with the former president—five thousand people had come to build one hundred homes in the short span of five days. Ken served as Carter's assistant in a forty-person crew whose mission was to build an eleven-hundred-square-foot residence for Wade and Charlena Gibson and their two children, a low-income family. "The first morning we showed up at six-thirty and found nothing but a concrete slab," recalls Ken.

We had to put up the whole framing on a day when it was 106 degrees at six-thirty in the morning. We heard a radio station announce that it would be the hottest day in Houston since 1936. We just started swinging our hammers and putting up the sides of this house. By eight in the morning, I thought I was dying. I didn't know how I could continue. Two feet away from me, Jimmy Carter was not even flinching, just hammering away. And this work is not like hammering together a bookshelf for half an hour. When you're not used to hammering more than fifteen minutes and your arm starts to vibrate after an hour, it's hard. Carter was on his knees, hammering in the foundation! I kept thinking, Where does he get this energy from?

By ten in the morning I had found a place to hide and pour cans of water over my head. I was afraid I'd have a stroke. But Carter hadn't even taken a break; by then he was up on a stepladder hammering in the structure for the roof to go on. He just didn't stop. Everything he wore—long-sleeve shirt, long pants, everything—was absolutely soaked with sweat after the first fifteen minutes.

At four o'clock in the afternoon, we were cutting two-by-fours and there was a long line to use the power saw. "No problem," said Carter, "I'll do it by hand." He spent the whole afternoon in the blistering sun cutting two-by-fours by hand. I don't know if you know how tiring that is. And it went on the whole week like this. I felt like I was in a biblical myth.

I couldn't figure out where Jimmy Carter and all the other people were getting their energy from.

By midweek Ken was getting to know some of the people on the work site. A young couple was there on their honeymoon; another couple was spending their two-week vacation from jobs at an RV factory in Indianapolis. "What every one of those five thousand people had in common was this: every one of them knew they felt better about themselves and their lives when they took a chunk of who they were and gave it to those less fortunate. This is a lot different from writing a check. It's a piece of your life, a piece of your energy, a piece of your soul, really."

By Friday morning, Ken remembers, the house looked nowhere close to being finished. It was still about 110 degrees in the shade. Then Jimmy Carter announced that they would finish the house by 2:30 in the afternoon.

The rest of us just gave each other knowing looks. Not by a long shot, we thought. But by 2:29 we were standing in the fully carpeted living room with the light fixtures working and the air conditioner on. All forty of us were standing in a circle in a small room, pretty close to each other. We'd just put in the most physically unbearable days most of us could remember, and we were a mess. We realized that we were strangers who had come together to build a house for Wade and Charlena Gibson. Then Jimmy Carter said to the couple, "First of all, I'd like you to look around at all the faces of the people who have given a part of who they are so you can have this new home." He took out this white linen bible—I'd never seen a book more beautiful—and he said, "I'd like to give this to you as the first book for your new home." Then he said to Wade, "Wade, when you look at the faces of the people who have built your home, how does it feel?" Wade, this big tough guy with his initials inscribed on one of his front teeth, looked around the room, and his face just exploded in tears. He reached out and put his arms around Carter, and everybody in the room started to cry.

For Ken Dychtwald, his Habitat for Humanity experience certified the wisdom that Jimmy Carter had imparted to him:

> You can get so caught up in your own family, career, and circle of friends that you believe everything you could ever want will come from just squeezing more juice out of those things. Now I know that when you reach further out to help people, the universe will reach out and continue to help you. Even to this day, most of what happens that's good in my life or in my business comes from other people helping me in an unselfish way. You can bet I'm going to continue helping other people as best I can.

Service Will Take You Places

"Only a life lived for others is a life worthwhile," said Albert Einstein. In service we come full circle. Helping others and sharing the hard-won skills and wisdom of our experience completes the hero's journey. Not only do we find that opening our hearts and lives will take us to amazing places; we also learn that service will take us to places we would never find by any other route. Whether it is Jim Zuberbuhler's ability to find moments of clarity or Jimmy Carter's stamina in swinging a hammer for endless hours on a hot day, our strengths seem to multiply as we use them to benefit others.

There remains one final step in the process of adventure. As the circle draws near completion, we are provided with a new experience: perspective on all that has passed before our eyes and within our hearts. Once we are back on familiar footing, it is time to bask a while in the warm glow of completion and enjoy the view.

After returning home from my horse trip in Patagonia, I found my own quest coming full circle. Wandering had been a perfect pastime, but it couldn't last a lifetime. I started putting my heart into my work and political causes in my own neighborhood. I became a better friend and teacher. Soon I was to begin a career whose rigors would, to my surprise, demand every skill I had ever gained.

The disciplines of speaking and writing, telling my tales in order to make their lessons useful to others, have become my service. The large chunk of my life spent on airplanes and in airports, separate from loved ones, frequently alone and often exhausted, is my sacrifice. It has also become my greatest satisfaction. Through it all, I still carry Rivera's teaching with me as my personal mantra: *There is nowhere to go, and nothing to do, except to be of service.*

Service was one of the lessons I learned from my stay with my gaucho *compañero*. But there was another teaching as well. Rivera's real genius was finding delight where others saw only deprivation. He helped me see that it is a good thing to laugh hard and often at the very strangeness of life.

Make Your Own Adventures

1. Focus on What Matters

Focusing on what matters allows us to live a more energized and meaningful life—and nothing matures a person's focus like a glimpse of his or her own mortality. Of all the exercises in perspective that I offer to clients in corporate settings, the following has always proven the most revealing. It helps people become a little more intimate with their own mortality while not actually risking more than a paper cut.

> *Fold a piece of paper into horizontal thirds and write the number "3" in the upper left-hand corner of each third. Now imagine the following scenario: A doctor has just told you that you have three years left to live. The prognosis is infallible, and in this exercise you can't get a second opinion. Place the word "years" next to the number 3 in the top third, and take a few minutes to ponder before writing a few answers to the following questions: What would you do? Where would you go? With whom would you spend your time?*
>
> *Then, on the second third of the paper, imagine that your prognosis has gotten much worse. Write the word "months" after the number 3. Take a deep breath and write about what would be essential to accomplish in your last ninety days on earth. Good.*
>
> *Finally, imagine that your condition has become much worse than before. Write "days" after the number 3 on the last third of the page, and write down what you would hope to do in the last few days of this incarnation.*

Responses from hundreds of participants in this exercise are fairly universal: as the time before one's imaginary death decreases, the emphasis placed on healing or renewing relationships increases. When people think seriously about what they would focus on if they knew the "long term" was becoming irrevocably short, guess what: those stock options become a whole lot less important than making peace or reaffirming love with spouses, parents, children, and friends.

What surprises some people is the fact that this focus on relationships is also the key to lasting success even when Father Time is not breathing down your neck. "Top firms do as well as they do because they are constantly hard at work building coherence among widely diverse, often conflicting interests," says Robert H. Waterman Jr. in *What America Does Right: Learning from Companies That Put People First*. "It's like a good marriage. A couple lives happily ever after because they work at making it work: a labor of love, but labor nonetheless." Whether you're involved in a Himalayan trek, an Internet start-up, or a nuclear family, the message is the same: the odds favor those who place as much importance on immediate relationships as they do on long-term material outcomes.

2. PRACTICE CPR AT WORK

While common sense and a flood of books on organizational psychology reinforce the importance of healthy human relations in the workplace, the adventure really begins when we put this awareness into practice. Here's another little paper-folding exercise that will take you from the theoretical to the practical in the matter of improving relationships at work.

> *For the next month, begin each working week by dividing a piece of paper into thirds. Write the letters C, P, and R in turn on each third:*
>
> C = COMPASSION
>
> P = PARTICIPATION
>
> R = RECOGNITION
>
> *List all the action steps you can think of to foster these three elements in your workplace. Make it happen. Look back at the week's end and see how well you have done.*

To get you started, here are a few ideas for action steps in each of the categories.

Compassion

- *Practice full-face management.* Forget one-minute managing. Real relationships require real time, and effective communication can't be multitasked. Listen in order to comprehend before you respond. If you allow all the time it takes to hear people out, you'll find that you save time overall because you're not patching up misunderstandings and conflicts later.

- *Don't lose that loving feeling.* Take time to reflect on the virtues, faults, problems, and unique characteristics of your co-workers as if they were family, and spend a few moments silently honoring each one with your deepest respect and care. Repeat this meditation on a regular basis, and you'll see the quality of your work relationships improving regardless of the difficulties you face on the job.

  What's love got to do with work? Everything. Green Bay Packers coach Vince Lombardi said: "Love is loyalty. Love is teamwork. Love and respect the dignity of the individual. Heartpower is the strength of your corporation." When General H. Norman Schwarzkopf was asked how he wanted to be remembered, he replied: "That he loved his family. That he loved his troops. And that they loved him." Love is not a superfluous or sentimental indulgence. It's the glue that holds an organization together.

- *Adopt an employee.* Become a mentor to an individual on your team with whom you have a natural affinity. Let him or her know that you're available to answer questions and offer on-the-job coaching. Show an unselfish, collaborative interest in advancing another's career. Becoming a coach will increase your team's overall effectiveness and sharpen your own job skills while you reap the psychic (and karmic) benefits of helping others.

Participation

- *Host a group vision quest.* Create a forum for people to discuss their highest goals for themselves and the organization. Take charge just long enough to share your own vision as a way to inspire everyone to do the same. Encourage individuals to speak about the importance of the work they do. Is there a common dream? Once you have developed a shared statement of purpose, publish it, display it, make it a part of the culture. Remember: it may be up to you to take action and overcome the forces of cynicism and fear. People thirst for a common purpose yet often need a strong personality to serve as catalyst.

- *Start a university.* Encourage employees to start a weekly brown-bag lunch series where different individuals present areas of expertise. Make the program the responsibility of the participants. The lunches can provide "best practice" sessions, offering valuable work-related skills, or simply serve as a venue for participants to share their own particular extracurricular expertise. With an emphasis on novelty and the enjoyment of all involved, these events will deepen a sense of community while broadening the knowledge base of all involved.

- *Organize an "everything you wanted to know but were afraid to ask" event.* Set aside the time and space for a no-holds-barred, penalty-free Q&A session for your team. Collect anonymously written queries to read aloud and discuss, or start in with questions like: Any good rumors making the rounds? Any pet peeves? Make sure not to get defensive. I got this idea from my friend John Polumbo who, as former president of Excite Inc., would sometimes walk into a meeting and announce that instead of "blabbing" for the next hour, he would just take questions. "Suddenly, the people in the room were writing the agenda." Take an hour to shed some light, open lines of communication, spread some empowerment—and enjoy a few chuckles along the way.

Recognition

- *Praise everyday heroes.* Create a process for naming a Hero of the Month. Pass out "Caught in the Act" nomination forms. Whenever someone spots a colleague rising above and beyond the call of duty, invite that person to note it on the form and hand it in. A panel of volunteer judges declares the winner, to be announced each month at a meeting or in a newsletter. Prizes should be imaginative: the president does the hero's job from that person's office while the hero gets the head office for a day.

- *Reward personal bests.* Instead of fostering competition among co-workers, foster cooperation by rewarding "personal bests." Design a system so that individuals can track their own performance over a period of time, based on mutually agreed standards. Whenever someone exceeds his or her previous record, it's time to recognize that person.

- *Commit small acts of kindness.* Nothing replaces the spontaneous pat on the back and the genuine expression of gratitude. Although systematic and public displays of recognition are effective, an underlying culture of appreciation is essential. Be generous in the moment, with kind words and supportive gestures. Model appreciation and encourage others to do the same.

3. HEED THE CALL

The problems of the world that seem far too big for us to change—much less solve—offer opportunities for us to discover how much more we are capable of than we imagine. "Life is trouble," said Kazantzakis' Zorba the Greek. "I hitch up my pants and go out looking for trouble." Sometimes it is incumbent on every human being to do the same.

> *Choose one big problem or crisis outside your work environment—hunger, pollution, economic discrimination—anything you have previously thought important but too big for you to do anything about. Heed the call to action by focusing on a part of the problem you can affect through local action.*

Few of us imagine we could lift a car off a child or pull a fellow climber out of a crevasse until unexpected circumstances call upon us to do it. Whatever larger-than-life crisis you choose to address, view it through this same lens of immediacy: the child is under the wheel and you are the only person around. Never mind that the problem is much more complicated and widespread; it's your motivation that counts. Jimmy Carter hasn't solved the entire problem of homelessness by promoting Habitat for Humanity, but he's actually put some people into homes and inspired thousands of others to get similarly involved. In the same way, neither you nor the world will ever be the same after your efforts.

Heeding the call makes us more caring and effective individuals at work and everywhere else, regardless of whether the world gets saved in the long run. When asked why she kept ministering to the poor when the problem obviously overwhelmed her resources, Mother Teresa replied, "We are not here to be successful. We are here to be faithful." What we can all be faithful to is our own humanity.

THE SIXTH STEP

Enjoy the View

When you arise in the morning

give thanks for the morning light,

give thanks for your life and strength,

And give thanks for the joy of living.

—OSAGE INDIAN PRAYER

KATE PRUEFER

*With my daughter Yeshe at home
in Idyllwild, California*

CHAPTER 11

The Adventure at Home

When people ask me nowadays what my latest big adventure is, I'm not always honest. Too often, in fact, I choose the low road and make something up.

"Soon I'll be off to retrace the ancient Silk Road through the mountains of Kyrgyzstan," I boast, or, "I'm leaving to track the hoofprints of Butch Cassidy and Sundance across the Old Bandit Trail in Patagonia." Both of which I will do, if I ever find the time. But for the moment—and I think it's going to be a long moment—I am fully occupied with the tasks of fatherhood and hustling enough peanuts to feed the family menagerie.

The challenge of becoming a patient and loving parent while battling the sleep deprivation induced by my two children's non-stop marathons of midnight colic, colds, and tantrums surpasses any challenge I've met in the wild or the developing world. I've had days recently when a straightforward fall off a mountain pass or drowning in the icy waters of Lake Titicaca sound like enviable alternatives to just hanging in there at home.

But every now and then when I'm asked about my current

Big Adventure, the truth sneaks out. "I'm . . . p-parenting," I stammer.

If the look on my questioner's face reveals disappointment, I have a ready comeback: "You don't have kids, do you?"

"I have a cat," is a popular response.

And my Uncle Ralph had hemorrhoids, I want to say. But even worse than those suffering from no-kids-naïveté are the folks who beam at me in confirmation: "Yes, isn't it wonderful? Parenting is the most wonderful adventure you will ever have."

I know adventures. They're terrifying, exhausting, unnerving, and humbling—but at least you get a break every now and then. There are base camps, snow caves, and seedy small-town bars to hunker down in and regroup. And sooner or later, you catch the bus or plane home to comfort, peace, and quiet. But parenting is the at-home adventure you can never escape.

Sure, a real adventure may leave you with nightmares from which you awaken in a chilly fright, awaiting the deadly roar of an avalanche. But then you hear the inner voice of calm and experience, telling you it was just a flashback. Compare that to toddler care, where you never wake from nightmares because you never get to sleep—and where your psyche has become so saturated with preschool videos that your inner wisdom speaks to you in a voice unnervingly like Kermit the Frog's.

Real adventures eventually come to an end; they don't have half-lives of a quarter of a century. Unlike high-altitude snowstorms, raging whitewater, or desiccating deserts, *kids don't even play fair.*

Worst of all is the discovery that I am not always the balanced, easygoing, resourceful kind of guy I have always believed myself to be. It's taken only five months for my infant son Jack to bring me to the verge of becoming a snarling Darth Vader. In such moments, from deep within I try to summon my "highest self," only to hear a profound whining: This is scary. I don't like this.

It's not fun anymore. I'm taking my toys and I'm going home. Then I realize that these aren't even my toys and I am home. And I recall a fragment of wisdom from my old amigo, El Loco Rivera: *There is nowhere to go.*

Mildly hung over from years of carrying my home in a backpack, I still entertain the illusion that I live a simple, elemental life. I drive a beat-up '87 Toyota pickup that refuses to die, live in a log home on a wooded ridgetop in a tiny town, and wear the same jeans and boots that carried me through the nineties. I sometimes arise at 5 A.M. to practice shamanic techniques taught to me by Eduardo Calderón: invoking the magic of the four directions and envisioning an enlightened life of courage, originality, and openness.

But other, less spiritual concerns consistently intrude on my consciousness. I seem to be falling victim to some kind of midlife virus that infects me with the desire to accumulate, acquire, invest, and remodel—in short, to become overtly middle class. I've even played golf and voted Republican (once each). Worst of all, I am no longer violently opposed to making a little money.

Fortunately, the primitive in me refuses to die. In truth, the quest for a respectable income makes me feel more Stone Age than middle-aged. I love the thrill of the hunt; these days it is called "marketing," but the essence of the quest remains unchanged. Regress with me for a moment, and you'll see what I mean.

Early Man as Family Man

I start the morning with a Paleolithic ritual of imbibing strong drink made from magic beans soaked in hot water. The resultant black and bitter potion provides me with my sense of omnipotence and energetic dreams. Clutching my cup in the part of my cave I call the office, I contemplate the mastodon tracks I saw yesterday above the valley and sniff the scrap of lion fur I picked from the bramble patch. (Granted, it may look like I'm just reviewing my phone and e-mail messages.)

Then I ponder the frost on the distant hill and think about laying in a supply of meat, dry firewood, and buffalo hides for the season ahead. Which is to say, I contemplate the follow-up calls I need to make today to potential clients, realizing that it's time to somehow scrape up enough cash to pay quarterly taxes and fatten our 401k.

Shuffling deeper into the cave in the half-light of dawn, I trip over a strangely shaped figurine. It's shaped like a female of my species yet has weirdly thin arms and wears a bright fabric with a symbolic rune on its chest. Why, it's Cheerleader Barbie! My eyes focus on a veritable battle scene of brightly colored plastic toys and stuffed animals littering the floor. There's Tinky Winky the Teletubby, Wakko the Animaniac, an assortment of Legos and Tinkertoys, unslunk Slinkies and hardened balls of Play-Doh, and a half-empty sippy-cup on its side dripping apple juice onto the carpet.

"Unnh," I grunt knowingly. Early Man has rediscovered his living room and wonders vaguely why he can't protect it from pillaging by the same band of primitives day after day. Soon this chamber will fill with the plaintive wails of my noble offspring, drowned out sporadically by the numbing ditties sung by a purple dinosaur. In response I will pound my chest and roar the fearsome cry of the alpha male—then I will pick up the toys and start running errands.

But tomorrow will be different, for tomorrow I hunt.

In fact, tomorrow I undertake the biggest hunting trip of the year. Heading in the direction of the sunrise, I will roam beyond the familiar wooded hilltops and the desert beyond to a place called Palm Springs. There I will hitch a ride on a metal sky-bird larger and faster even than the ancient pterodactyl, and it will bear me to the mythical realm known as Atlantis (Atlanta to you) for a ritual rendezvous attended by thousands of warriors from the Life Insurance Salesmen tribe.

You see, I have been selected to be among the bards, jesters, and storytellers to stand before their huge campfire and cast a spell with my tales of true adventure. If I am successful in capturing the horde's attention, I will soon have access to the biggest source of buffalo hides on the planet and gain great respect among the Make-Money-with-Our-Mouths tribe to which I belong.

This trip to Atlanta is big. You hear about the influential Million-Dollar Round Table from the moment you begin speaking. "It will make you or break you" is the friendly conventional wisdom. "Why, I know a guy who spoke at MDRT and was such a hit that he never had to worry about a thing for the rest of his life. Today he owns several small countries in Europe. Traces it all back to that one speech . . . ," and so on.

Like entertainers, entrepreneurs, and ambitious cavemen, professional speakers are always looking for the big break. That's the event that catapults you into the hearts and minds of conventioneers and makes you a household name, maybe even a powerfully effective agent of constructive change in corporate society. By the way, it's the same big break that allows you to substantially up your fee. Higher fees mean a better living, of course, but above all they mean less traveling. The irony is not lost on me: after years of satisfying my wanderlust, I have come to view success as having the means to stay at home more often.

The convention hotel is huge; my room is small. It appears to be exactly the same room I have stayed in before every speaking engagement for the last five years. How did they get it here? I wonder. At least the sameness of it all allows me to concentrate on rehearsing my stories. The trick is to bring them alive again with every delivery. No matter how familiar the tales of Titicaca, Mount Fitzroy, and Eduardo the Healer have become for me, they are new to every audience. They comprise the personal mythology that I share with everyone I hope to entertain and inspire.

My reflection is broken by the realization that the same fellow who's been following me around the country—the one who always plays the TV too loud and long into the night—has once again booked the room next to mine. My mind, still on California time, finally lets my body drift into sleep some time around midnight. Unfortunately that's 3 A.M. in Atlanta, and my wake-up call comes at 5. No problem—that's the same sleep pattern I have at home! So what if I have to deliver the biggest talk of my life on two hours of sleep. After all, I've endured worse on the windswept steppes of Patagonia—or have I?

A few hours later I'm standing at a designated spot for greeting passersby, my name tag and smile firmly pasted on, pressing the flesh and exchanging bleary, early-morning pleasantries. My ribbon reading "Main Platform" makes me an instant celebrity. Though no one has actually ever heard of me, attendees treat me as if I am General Colin Powell. I puff out my chest and try to look the part; every shaman is part showman, after all.

By midmorning I'm sitting in the front row of the audience in Atlanta's huge Civic Center. The other speakers are truly incredible; they mesmerize, they entertain, they are received by thunderous standing ovations. It appears that the careers of my tribesmen are made. Good for them!

When my turn comes, I feel reasonably confident. I know my show is a good one, and I have walked this kind of tightrope often enough to trust my balance even if the wind blows up from out of nowhere. I do, however, face one sizable challenge: at the client's request, I've had to condense my ninety-minute show into half the time. That means sacrificing some adventures in order to leave untouched the crown jewel of my presentation: a surefire musical medley of bagpipes, drums, and angelic music accompanying a photographic portfolio of the faces of friends I've made around the world. That's always a winner.

Oh yes, there's one more glitch. The production company has just advised that without bothering to consult me, someone has made a unilateral decision to remove all my text slides. This someone decided that those slides were "tedious" and I have them memorized anyway, right? Well, of course! I am seconds away from being called to the stage, still in shock at the removal of the text slides, when someone hands me a headset.

"Sorry, Dr. Salz," an anonymous voice buzzes in my ears. "The rear projector has just gone on the blink. It's just the weirdest thing. What we will have to do is project your slides for only part of the time. You don't mind not having have your slides up the whole time you're talking, do you?"

I wince, but before I can compose a response I hear the moderator's voice booming through the cavernous hall: "So please welcome Dr. Jeff Salz!" I climb the steps to the stage amid a wave of unearned applause. The view is of a glowing sea of faces extending outward seemingly forever, filling rows, balconies, and boxes. Reeling from the last-minute change-ups, I stumble through a clumsy initial attempt to build rapport, amazed that things are going okay. Not great, but okay. A few minutes in, I can feel "the ripple" beginning—the energetic melding of the audience's mind with my meaning that is the speaker's ultimate goal and aphrodisiac. I'm only on the ten with ninety yards left to the goal line, but the ball is firmly in my possession and there is plenty of time on the clock.

"Now let's go to slides," I say cheerily. The room darkens. I remove the wireless remote from my pocket and press the button. Nothing happens.

I try again. Nothing. Then the first slide finally appears. "Okay!" I laugh awkwardly. Then the second slide flashes up, immediately followed by the third. I struggle to catch up but the slides keep advancing as if the projector has a life of its own. Opportunities to tell my best stories vanish as images appear and disappear on the huge screens at random.

Perspiration drips from my brow while it's raining sweat inside my expensive suit. I feel like Houdini unable to escape from a padlocked sauna while five thousand people stare. Unaware of the behind-the-scenes technical catastrophes, the audience probably shares a single thought: this guy is not so good!

When the final slide appears, I can't tell if my forty-minute presentation has taken ten minutes or ten seconds. Thank God for the stirring finish; I cue the musical sequence and some clapping follows. I am done.

Afterward, large crowds swirl around all the other speakers. They are obviously being congratulated and hired on the spot for lucrative engagements in exotic places, after which they will retire in luxury. I stand alone, grinning foolishly, trying to make sense of what just happened. The production team has apologized profusely; it seems that the remote control had stopped working so they focused a camera with a long-distance lens on my thumb and advanced the slides whenever it seemed to twitch. Apparently, I was twitching quite a lot. Oh, well, there was nothing to do but graciously accept the apologies.

Finally I notice a woman in a sharp business suit striding purposefully toward me. When she sticks out her hand, I cannot help but notice from the rainbow of ribbons affixed to her name tag that she is a big player. It's not the quantity of connections, it's the quality, I think hopefully. Something good will come of this; Early Man will bring home the slain mastodon—or at least a little package of bacon—after all.

"Excuse me," she says.

"Hi! What can I do for you? Did you enjoy the show?"

"It was nice," she says flatly. "I'm sorry, but I just had to ask. What was that really weird music?"

Back with the Clan of the Stuffed Bears

Home again, 5 A.M. Time once more for the energizing black brew while I lick the wounds earned in Atlanta and try to sniff the winds for new and lucrative scents. Alone in the darkness, I fire up the laptop, check out my e-mail, and get to work. These are the few and precious moments that I jealously guard in order to get some creative work done before the day's hubbub begins.

No sooner do I get started than there comes a scratching at my office door. It is my daughter Yeshe, a blond waif in cat pajamas rubbing the sleep from her eyes with tiny fists.

"Is it seven o'clock yet?" she purrs demurely, knowing full well it is not. Seven o'clock is wake-up time; my watch says 6:15. I've lost this battle so many times that I immediately capitulate. I warm Yeshe's morning milk, then park her in front of the television in my office to watch Barney's *Camp WannaRunnAround* for the umpteenth time.

"Remember, when you're with your friends and family every day is a special day!" says the fuzzy purple prehistoric reptile. Yeshe stares at the screen, transfixed. I am humming along involuntarily, battling myself to keep from breaking out into another Barney hit that will cue up momentarily: "A-Hiking We Will Go." I had no idea that kids could watch the same thing over and over. The good news is that this compulsion keeps Yeshe hooked for at least a little while. The bad news is that my subconscious has been completely reprogrammed by the singsongy mantras of the Toddler Gods.

At 6:45 the intercom on my desk buzzes. I hear Kate's weary voice asking if I'll come upstairs and fetch baby Jack so she can catch a few moments of peace. The poor kid's first encounter with a head cold means that Jack alternated between sniffling and screaming all night while Kate and I traded off running back and forth to his crib. I grabbed some sleep in fits and starts.

Battling several thousand years of maternal programming embedded in her DNA, Kate was less successful. No wonder she is fatigued. I tote the bundle of spew and drool and milk-soaked pajamas that represents my heritage and insert him, squirming and mewing, into the saucer-shaped plastic activity wheel at my feet.

"Yeshe, please don't stick your feet in Jack's face."

"But he likes to put them in his mouth and suck on them. Watch, Daddy!"

"I don't want to watch. Just stop it. He'd suck on Ricky the goldfish if it got anywhere near his mouth."

"Can I get the fish? Can I? I want to see."

"No, that was just an *example*."

"But you said I could. Waaaaah!!"

Eight o'clock. Kate groggily descends the stairway, wearing an oversized Mets baseball shirt. I think about her conversation with Kent the spa guy. She'd asked him to fix the hot tub at a friend's cabin where we were planning a romantic weekend get-away, and they'd ended up commiserating about the challenge of maintaining passion in long-term relationships. Thinking like a guy, Kent advised Kate: "Wear something sexy. You know, the kind of stuff you put away a long time ago."

When she told me the story, we both laughed. Every night when we crawl wearily into bed at 9 P.M. it feels like long past midnight. It wouldn't matter who was in bed with us or what they were wearing. The only thing either of us have felt passion-ate about for weeks has been the feel of a soft pillow on our cheeks: foreplay to a few hours of uninterrupted sleep.

Now I notice my wife in the morning light as it slants in through the windows. Suddenly Kate looks beyond lovely in her rumpled Mets uniform. Our intimate, peculiar journey through the world is steadily drawing us ever closer, into a deep and easy affection that's been thoroughly battle-tested and childproofed over time. I can hardly wait till Friday night at the cabin.

Noticing the shift in my attention, Yeshe gives up on *Camp WannaRunnAround* and leaps on my lap, nuzzling my face and twirling a finger in my beard. For the moment she ceases to be the growly, scratching lion cub and is content to look up at me sweetly. I gaze down at her pale skin, rosebud lips, and clear eyes in wonder. I have never seen anything more beautiful. I can scarcely believe she is my daughter.

Jack has quieted too. My son, Jack Salz: Mini-Me. I recall the time I held him in my outstretched hands and, looking down into his eyes, seemed to be looking back at myself through his eyes. It reminded me of Carmine's Barber Shop when I was a kid. Carmine had mirrors on both walls, front and back. I would crane my neck and peer into the endless reflections, further and further into infinity. I smile at Jack now and he smiles back, starts waving his arms. In that second my entire being fills with a love that is indescribable. There are simply no words for it. Before me is a tiny creature I would die for without hesitation. But more important, he is someone I am living for every day.

If we reach this life's pinnacle when we finally feel that another's welfare is more important than our own, these moments given us by our children are the greatest gifts of a lifetime. The next time Darth Vader rears up inside me, I know he won't last long. For even the faintest residue of the immense love I am feeling now will melt him in a heartbeat.

"Looks like you're doing okay," Kate says with a knowing smile.

I nod and look around. At least for the moment, I've conducted this outlandish band to a crescendo of playing in happy unison. I've even been able to put a few good thoughts on paper, and the work leads I jotted down suddenly look a whole lot more promising. This is clearly the greatest challenge I have ever faced: to balance partnering, parenting, earning a living, and doing creative work while never giving up on making a positive difference in the world.

In fact, any one of these challenges is as tough as scaling a mountain, fording a river, traversing a desert, or breaking the culture barrier with the natives in an exotic, faraway land. But I've never before encountered an adventure as complicated and demanding as taking on all these challenges at once. You've got to have balls to juggle. I guess I have more balls than I ever imagined.

I set down my coffee cup. Outside the window above my desk, past the business books, family photos, and Maximón with his cigar, the jagged 10,000-foot peaks of the San Jacinto Mountains glow in the morning light. For me, adventure has finally come home; I know there is no place on earth I would rather be. Before I can stop it, I hear that inner nasal singsongy voice again. Something about me loving you . . . You loving me . . . And us being a happy family.

"You know, Kate," I call into the kitchen, "did you ever stop to think that Barney is an enlightened being?"

CHAPTER 12

Live beyond the Peak Moment

njoying the view is the last essential step of adventure and
the first step into the rest of your life. For if we live only
to achieve a "peak moment," there is nothing to do afterward
but wax nostalgic, feeling sad that ordinary life just doesn't
measure up. In fact, adventure should be a means to put the joy
back into our lives—a way to reinvigorate the experience of
"human being" when daily life may have become a grind.

Begin with Celebration

Putting the joy back into life begins with celebration. When
you've reached a literal or metaphoric mountaintop after an
arduous climb, the next step is really a two-step. There is something about the top of the world that makes people want to
dance. Silly as it seems, a jig of joy seems to placate the mountain gods and does our own souls some good at the same time.
Some philosophers argue that celebration is the highest form of
worship, the ultimate expression of humankind. All I can tell
you is that it's the only thing that feels right.

Continue with Gratitude and Reflection

It is always good to say thanks and express our appreciation for life, even if at times we are not certain whom we should address. "Saying grace" sincerely is a way of recognizing the grace inherent in our lives and opens our heart like few other expressions.

After celebration and gratitude it is time for reflection: the deep examination of all that we have seen in order to see more deeply into all that follows. As Rene Dumal reminds us in *Mount Analogue:* "There is an art of finding one's direction in the lower regions by the memory of what one saw higher up. When one can no longer see, one can at least still know." The little things we master—topping the mountain, completing the project, producing the work of art—all contribute to our mastery of life, which might be summed up as the knowledge that existence is profoundly good and so are we. This is the celebratory inspiration that we gather along the trail and save in the heart's cache for retrieval in our hours of greatest need.

The big view is always available to us, whether we're reaching a mountain's peak on a once-in-a-lifetime quest or rounding the corner in the financial district on the way to work on just another workday. *Seeing life from a heightened perspective is a matter of attitude, not altitude.*

Seek Aliveness and Joy

Why do we seek the mountaintop in the first place? Because it is there, as the old saying goes? My own peak-seeking experience has taught me just the opposite: that human beings climb mountains because something is not there. Something is missing, and we will literally climb walls to find it.

Mountaineering is a metaphor of journeying toward heaven while descending ever deeper into ourselves. Whether we seek self-respect, illumination, or glory, we climb in a search for missing pieces of ourselves. We climb to recapture lost aliveness and joy.

In my journal a few days after the accident on FitzRoy, I wrote, "There is power in me, for I am the survivor. But for how long will I survive? Until my own time comes, I have to live out all that is the best of me. That much I owe Steve and myself. Because to live without a song and a dance is not to live at all, really. The commitment of the mountaineer is to pursue whole-heartedly and to know whole-soulfully the man-shaped essence that he is."

Contrary to popular belief, climbing is the route to fulfilling not a death wish but a life wish. The taste of danger reawakens us to what truly matters. In an article in *Men's Journal*, "The Joy of Danger," Sebastian Junger wrote of a close call he shared with some journalist pals during the Balkans conflict:

And there it was again: that wild slamming in the chest, that sudden certainty that there was no life I wanted to be living except this very one, right here, right now. It wasn't the degree of risk, which was surprisingly minimal—it was the idea of it. It was the fact, for a moment, at least, we had no way of knowing what would happen. And when nothing did—when our lives were handed back to us exactly as they had been before, and we were laughing and talking and we switchbacked along the steep coast—it was as if we'd been introduced to the world all over again. And for a while, we saw the world as it really was: a fascinating, seemingly limitless place for us to explore as fully as possible. That's the reason to take risks. Otherwise, you don't truly understand what you have to lose.

Stop the World and Get On

There aren't many old mountain climbers. Some die with their boots on, of course. For the lucky majority, their desire to risk life and limb falls away before they do. My friends tell me that getting married and having kids has put about forty years on my life. It's certainly true that my challenges these days are more often off the rock than on. And when I do find myself a few hundred feet up a slick stone face, ready to make a dicey move, I think twice and then a third time. How important is this particular three feet of granite when weighed against my daughter and son having a dad tomorrow? Is this heart-stopping moment possibly worth breaking the hearts closest to my own? Might not there be a way to live on the edge without risking life itself?

Eventually one has to stop depending on adrenaline and endorphins as the primary catalysts of a higher consciousness. Shamans, mystics, and meditators have always cultivated the ability to "stop the world" and rejuvenate their awareness without going anywhere but the deep recesses of their own minds and souls.

Do Nothing

Scholar and meditation teacher Alan Watts would talk about the importance of "doing nothing" every day. "The same way you have to stop talking long enough to have something worth talking about, and stop thinking long enough to know what's worth thinking about, you must spend some time each day doing nothing . . . Just watching and remembering how to live."

This disciplined approach to "enjoying the view" requires that we consecrate at least a small portion of our lives on a regular basis to lowering our sails in order to elevate our thinking. Joseph Campbell suggested that it is both possible and essential to undertake personal vision quests in the privacy of our own homes. "You must have a room, for a certain hour or so a day, where you don't know what was in the newspaper that morning, a place where you don't know who your friends are, you don't know what you owe anybody, you don't know what anybody owes you. This is a place where you can simply experience and bring forth what you are and what you might be."

Meditation Takes Many Forms

My problem is, I'm not a meditator. In fact, I'm a veritable menace to a room full of serious meditators. Not only am I unable to sit silently, clearing my head of the movie within, I can't even sit quietly in real life when I've got the wide-screen version playing right in front of me.

Leading treks to the Himalayas in the latter stage of my adventuring, I became enthralled by the local Buddhist culture. Unfortunately, after learning all the names of the principal figures on the walls of the monasteries and a handful of right precepts, all of Buddhism seemed to come down to sitting. And sitting a while longer. Not only would I never attain enlightenment, I realized, I was probably backpedaling through the wheel of life. I'd be lucky to reincarnate as a gnat.

But while others found inner peace sitting long hours in the chanting halls of the monasteries, I kept on stumbling into transcendent moments when I was anything but still: strolling along wooded paths by rushing waters, cresting high passes on an empty trail at dusk. Even my encounters with the locals—an impromptu dance in a tiny village at mid-day or laughing with the monks over yak butter tea in a monastery courtyard—took me to places of emotional and spiritual contentment that I couldn't even get close to while sitting cross-legged and immobile. I was perplexed.

The Lama's Lesson

One afternoon, I was able to pose my problem to an English-speaking lama in a small teahouse near the Sherpa settlement of Junbesi. It was a chance meeting at the tiny shack that sold sweet milk tea to weary travelers. I was on my way down the valley; the lama was on the way up. There was a sparkle in his eyes as he took my hand warmly in his and introduced himself as the lama in residence from the next monastery up the trail. He wore the gold and maroon robes of the Nyingma lineage. Two boy monks scurried about, tending to his needs. The only clients of the shopkeeper at that hour, the lama and I chatted politely. He seemed to enjoy practicing his language skills, recounting in British-accented English how he had been raised in this valley but had spent the last ten years studying in India. He was back now for good. India was too "agitating," he said. "I prefer the peace and quiet where I can meditate. Meditation is important."

Whether he was omniscient or simply noticed the look of dismay that must have clouded my face, he then asked, "You do meditate, don't you?"

My angst poured out as I decided to level with the lama. I told him of my proclivity for activity and my concern about reincarnating in the insect realm.

The lama chuckled. "Do you help others regularly?" he inquired.

"Yes, whenever I can," I replied.

"Do you endeavor to become less self-centered in daily action?"

I explained that I made every attempt to do so.

"Then it is possible that your life is your practice," proposed the lama with a steady gaze, "and your activity is your meditation."

Ever since my conversation with that lama, I have experienced a sense of deep relief. If I keep my head on straight and remember that looking out for number one is not my number one priority, I may yet catch a glimpse or two of the underpinnings of the universe without having to spend three hours a day in an empty room with my knees bent. I might not even be coming back as a gnat.

Secrets of a Visionary Consultant

When I met Michael Lindfield in St. Louis at an executive seminar, I immediately knew that I wanted to ask him his secrets. It's obvious that Michael is plugged in to something big; a remarkable light emanates from his intense and intelligent eyes and he always seems revved to the max with a purposeful energy. What was the view like from behind those eyes? I wondered. And how did an individual with such a diverse and freewheeling résumé find himself as a full-fledged executive in a giant corporation?

Michael's background is impressively eclectic. He has taught rock climbing and led wilderness adventures in the Scottish highlands. For five years he was the director of Findhorn, a visionary institution in Britain whose development of new models for education, community life, and interaction with the natural world has long inspired me. Michael also cofounded and directed a horticultural college in Scotland, managed a "technologies for sustainable living" exchange program in India, and wrote a book, *The Dance of Change*. Finally, he has been a senior organizational development consultant at the Boeing Corporation for the last decade.

When we got to talking, Lindfield and I discovered that we had a thing or two in common. We knew many of the same trails in the Himalayas. Where I had walked, however, often battling for breath, Michael had run. Running is something we both enjoy. I also enjoy stopping; Michael does not. Although Michael's daily practice includes sitting meditation, he revealed that marathons, ultramarathons, and endurance races are his true routes to revelation.

Michael describes the life-altering experience of the long-distance athlete:

> For me it's running from the inside out, as if it's really my soul in motion. As much as I can, I'm paying attention to my breathing and my form. Sometimes it's a struggle, especially in the twenty-four-hour runs when you have to draw upon resources you don't believe you have. As I'm running, I'll use different mantras; one that I call upon regularly is *I am running through life, life is running through me.*

While running a hundred-mile endurance race in the Sierra Nevadas, Michael hit a wall. Having completed nearly half the race, including most of a 4,000-foot gain in elevation, Michael became chilled, dehydrated, and unable to keep down food. "I thought I was going to die," he remembers. "My body started to shake and to shiver, I felt that I needed help right there and then. I sat down and thought, Oh my God, I've come so far . . . forty-six miles. But there were still fifty-five to go. I was about to give up. No, I thought. There is a way. But I need help."

Michael's help arrived from within his own consciousness. At the next aid station he found some tincture of ginger to drink and rub on an acupuncture point. That helped, but he also went to work on his energy reserve by reconnecting with what he calls "the spirit of life" outside his own body. "I pulled in the spirit to flood my body and brought it back to life. With every mile I made past the aid station, I began to get stronger and stronger. I made up two hours on my time in the last fifty-odd miles and felt fantastic. I was running through the night, strong, enjoying the stars, enjoying the whole experience. I felt like I'd been reborn."

Michael completed his hundred-mile run.

By the end of it I was feeling an incredible humility. I saw that whenever I feel something is impossible, that may be true from a limited perspective of my personal, finite resources. This limited-resource view is like thinking the body runs on a battery, and when the battery's dead, that's it. But I realized that I was not limited to plugging into a battery, but in fact the main power source! There is a life current continuously flowing through me that I'm not always accessing. I realized that the spirit of life can break through everything.

Cultivate Soft Strength

Michael saw further proof of this principle while running on a new blacktop path that had been laid down near his home.

After a few months, I could see these bumps in the pavement. Little bumps that got bigger and bigger, and one day they broke open. I stopped to see why and discovered that fiddler ferns were busting through the two-inch blacktop. I just stood there saying, "Yes!" That little scene reinforced my conviction that the force of life cannot be held back by any material obstacle. You wouldn't try to break up pavement with a fern, yet it was breaking through slowly and surely on its own. The force of life pushing gently, firmly, and relentlessly from the inside can move mountains. If you want to know where the real power lies, that's it: a soft, relentless strength.

The force of life pushing gently, firmly, and relentlessly from the inside can move mountains. I don't know about you, but I'm glad that Michael Lindfield has brought his insights and perseverance to corporate America.

Practice Controlled Folly

I love my buddy George. But I wasn't even supposed to like him. George Gorton was a Republican political consultant and campaign manager for former California governor Pete Wilson. George's successful efforts on behalf of a score of candidates—all conservative—had surely affected the face of the California political scene at a time when I considered even Democrats to be in league with the devil. I thought I was beyond politics; the only parties I supported were Libertarian and New Year's Eve.

A mutual friend had organized a dinner gathering partly to pit George and myself against each other like two fighting roosters. But the crowd was soon disappointed. After engaging in a nonstop idea-fest for an hour, we emerged with arms around each other, best of friends. We have remained so ever since. George bought an expedition parka and came trekking with me in the Himalayas. I rented a tuxedo and shook hands with Pete Wilson after George got him elected a second time.

Another of George's effective campaigns for controversial candidates was his recent stint as the leader of a team of American consultants in Russia running the presidential campaign of Boris Yeltsin. His mission: pull the incumbent out of a steadily worsening situation. Not necessarily the best choice for a president, Yeltsin was the only choice. Anarchy and the collapse of the entire democratic structure of the new Russia was the apparent alternative. Luckily for the free world, George Gorton is pretty good at what he does, and Yeltsin pulled off an amazing electoral comeback.

Regardless of his politics, George is one joyful guy. Gleeful exuberance is his most significant personality quirk, especially in the often unfunny world of politics. But I think that it's his very refusal to surrender to the pervasive seriousness all around him that makes him so successful.

George describes his basic MO as learning to practice controlled folly. He defines this approach to life as "managing to live in the world and being as appropriate as the world expects you to be, but at the same time recognizing it as complete folly. What the world expects of you doesn't have to impinge on your sense of freedom or personal joy."

To maintain his sense of joy, George practices his own brand of active meditation. "It is a simple exercise that can be done on an evening walk. You move your attention out of the part of your mind that calculates and thinks, and into the part of your mind that simply accepts sensory input." George dubs this technique *wow travel:*

When you suspend all thought and maximize your sensory perception, you find yourself turning the corner and saying, *Wow, look at that incredible tree*, instead of, *Gee, I wonder if I have enough money in the bank.* When I travel now, I build my itinerary to ensure the maximum number of wow experiences. I don't visit many museums or rush to see monuments like Notre Dame. I prefer to spend time in a little village and try to sink into the culture there, so that I learn what it would be like to live in this town, sitting on the curb like they do and eating the bread they eat. It's like sitting still long enough in the woods to see the animals come out around you, instead of just hiking through in a hurry. Wow travel reminds me of what's truly important. Elections can seem important when you're in the middle of them, as if the world will break or be healed because someone gets elected governor. When you practice wow travel you see that the trees and the birds and the planet go on much the same no matter who is elected. This restores some balance to your perspective.

Maintain Balance in Chaos

When we are well balanced we're less likely to be knocked off our center of gravity by extreme circumstances, such as those George Gorton encountered in Russia. "The people I met there on a daily basis in Russia were extremely powerful," he recalls, "and terribly arrogant. They were used to dealing with people as inferiors, using them and then throwing them out. These leaders were a tough bunch who tried to be very intimidating. And they often succeeded."

To keep his own balance under pressure, George practiced a secret, silent chant every morning as part of his daily meditation. Prior to important meetings, he would repeat this private invocation. "This allowed me to put myself and these intimidating people in perspective. I could walk in and look these guys in the eye and tell them exactly what I thought. They often answered sarcastically, and it was important that I not take the bait but keep pressing the theme of what they needed to do."

"Everyone can devise their own centering chant," George says. "Whether it is a scrap of song, a prayer from your religious faith, or just a personal affirmation, this chant can remind you that your world is much larger than the confines of the job or challenge you're facing. It will help you do your best."

Choose Gratitude

George has found that an attitude of gratitude is essential for maintaining a positive, energetic, and effective way of life.

People think they are subject to emotions that come over them uncontrollably. That is really not true. Once you have a little practice at it, you are able to pick and choose the emotions that you want to experience. There is a muscle for choosing emotions, just like any other muscle, and if you practice you can learn to choose gratitude more often than not. I've found that gratitude is one of the very best emotions I can experience for restoring my soul.

People create the stories of their lives by consciously or unconsciously selecting the filter through which they view life's experiences. Just as an optometrist flips various shapes and shades of lenses before our eyes before prescribing a pair of glasses, so can we choose the kind of glass through which we view the world. "You could look at any difficult challenge you've faced over the last six months and view it with dismay or gratitude," says George. "Those people who string together the most experiences of gratitude are filled with happiness and positive feelings toward themselves and the universe. This may sound Pollyannaish, but in fact I actually say to myself every day, 'Great things always happen to me. I'm blessed. My life is golden and I'm thrilled with it.' Gratitude generates the energy we call joy."

Joy, like adventure, is an inside job. Its presence or absence in our lives doesn't really depend on chance. As George Gorton says, joy is really a choice—a choice that requires both effort and a regularly renewed intention. Or, as author and artist J. Ruth Gendler wrote in *The Book of Qualities*, "Joy waits for us. Her desire to walk with us is as great as our longing to accompany her."

Stay Light and Graceful under Pressure

C. W. Metcalf is my instructor at SLU, the School of Lightening Up. He has spent too many years volunteering to help trauma victims and survivors in hospitals and hospices to confuse seriousness with solemnity. Speaker, author, consultant, and professional mirth-maker par excellence, this man of many talents felt his busy life come to a screeching halt recently as he lay face up in an emergency room. After flatlining from a brain hemorrhage, C. W. seemed proud to point out that he didn't have a near-death experience.

"It was a death experience," he says. "I was a dead puppy." The main artery in his brain had mysteriously torn loose, and instead of splitting and killing him instantly, it had twisted on itself and begun killing him pretty quickly. Ninety percent of his blood was flowing into his brain cavity; a 10 percent flow of blood to his brain was all that kept him alive. "And that's really all you need," C. W. reminds me, "to be a consultant."

> I could hear everything that was happening. I could hear the doctors and nurses talking and the machines going, and I heard one of them change from "beep, beep, beep," to something like "AaaaAaaaAaaaAaaa." How you're going to spell that, I don't know. Anyway, then I heard somebody say, "He's flatlined, get the paddles." I thought, isn't that interesting, I'm dead! What happened then I don't talk about very much. I've read all the books about being "saved by the light" and "dancing in the light," and I always thought that sounded like wishful thinking.
>
> What I can tell you is that my former writing partner— who had been dead for several years—wrapped his arms around me, gave me a big hug, and told me that the doctors were going to give me a shot. I woke up sitting on the table in the ER with an adrenaline needle buried in my chest. A nurse at the other end of it was staring at me, and I was staring right back. I didn't even know if I could speak, but I managed to choke out the words, "If I live I'll buy you guys another fibrillator." Then I passed out. When those words came out of my mouth I knew I was going to survive. The first lesson I'd learned from trauma survivors and kids in hospice is that one of the prime strengths of survivors is the

ability to appreciate absurdity. It's not just laughing off death or danger, but being able to look into the face of the monster and notice the wart at the end of its nose. Oddly enough, that gives you a sense of control over the circumstances.

C. W. flatlined twice more, but he is convinced that he survived because of skills he learned from people who had faced death and come out the other side.

One of those skills is a sense of humor—I don't mean joking around so much as staying light and graceful under pressure instead of tightening up or bearing down. My response to that nurse with the needle was no accident—it was an instinct that had been drilled into me by all the work I had done with people in catastrophic situations. I knew that if I said "God, please save me" or "Don't let me die!" I was going to be feeding the process of death. Instead, I decided I was going to feed the process of life. And you know what? I bought them another fibrillator.

Make a Joyful List

Another life-preserving skill of consciousness, C. W. adds, is a disciplined sense of joy in being alive. Competence in joy can be both instructed and acquired, he asserts. "Misery comes for free, you know. Suffering, pain, trauma—they're all too easy to acquire. A sense of lightness and joy is what we have to work at."

One of C. W.'s favorite teaching tools is a "joy list." The idea came to him from a young boy at a hospice who had compiled a list of all the fun he'd known in life. He had overheard his parents talking about how unfair it was that he was to die leaving so many wonderful things he would never do, so he compiled a list to make his parents feel better.

Whenever he was conscious, this boy labored under the hideous pressure of a brain stem tumor to write these things down. Twelve pages, 113 things written on both sides. The first thing on the list was "Uncle Harry's house, 1979 Christmas tree fire." I asked what was so funny about that, and he said, "Oh it was great! The tree caught on fire and Uncle Harry came in with the fire extinguisher and Aunt Marilyn said, " No, you'll ruin the new drapes!" And she grabbed the tree and hauled it through the living room and set everything on fire. And he's running behind her spraying everything and she's yelling, 'No, no! You'll ruin the furniture . . .' "

After hearing that story I tried to come up with my own joy list. At first I couldn't come up with very much. I started carrying around a pocket memo book, and every time something made me laugh or nourished my sense of joy I would write it down. Now I have a file drawer full of those pads. Now I tell my audiences to give the joy list a try for six weeks, writing down everything that uplifts them. When people start making notes, they begin to realize how much joy is in their lives that would otherwise be forgotten.

For example, I'm standing in my yard right now talking to you on the phone and I am incredibly grateful that anybody cares what I think. I've got my pad sitting on the table and I've just written down today's date and "conversation with Jeff Salz." That's all I need. Later, I'll recall this conversation and appreciate how funny you are . . . and, of course, how much funnier I am. And that will make a real difference in my life!

Find What You Seek

What we seek we tend to find. When we learn to observe ourselves with a joyful and humorous eye, we discover no shortage of material. Learning what makes us laugh, we find others laughing along with us. Instead of living life as an obligation, we learn to play—seriously.

"Humor is a serious way of being that you can consciously develop," remarks C. W. Metcalf. "As you develop it, you are strengthening your ability to remain creative and flexible under pressure. You are becoming a problem solver rather than a problem. A sense of joy in being alive is crucial; most physicians will tell you that joy is always an element in what they call 'the will to live.' If you don't love being alive, why try to stay here when the going gets tough?"

I am told I laugh a lot. Anything from the terrifically twisted to the mildly madcap keeps my laughometer torqued, but some level of levity is required for me to function normally. According to my wife, Kate, I get pretty pesky when I'm off my "medication"—that is, when I've somehow forgotten to laugh at one of life's more challenging absurdities. She describes my philosophy as "if it is not fun, it is not worth doing."

The fact that I insist on always prioritizing the zany and playful is one reason it has taken me twenty years to write this book. It is also one reason our lives are so interesting. And it's the reason that my kids will never have to worry about looking more foolish than their father.

Insist on Joy

We can find happiness—and the deepest, most lasting kind of success—whenever we start living with a deliberate intent to enjoy the view. Luckily, joy is a discipline that is enjoyable to learn, apply, and practice. Not a bad job if you can get it. From this adventurer's point of view, that's exactly the job we've got.

To insist on joy does not mean doing anything different. It may require, however, doing everything differently. To really

enjoy life requires a dedicated effort to every step in this book—
from leaping in faith to aiming for the heights, from giving our
all to invoking our imaginations and opening our hearts. Only
this way will we assure ourselves the reinforcing glimmers of
gladness that make a long trip possible.

"It's being in love with the process, excited by the process,
that matters," says deep-sea explorer Bob Ballard. "If all you seek
is a reward at the end, it's drudgery all along the way. You've
missed the game. You've missed the joy."

Loren Eiseley once found himself prodding a spider's web
with a pencil, pondering what the world might look like at that
moment to the spider. It was unlikely, surmised the naturalist,
that the spider was thinking, "Oh, my gosh. Here is Loren
Eiseley, poking my web with a pencil." Far more likely, the tiny
creature was caught up in some spider version of reality inspired
by past experience and bounded by a spider's limits of perception.

Like that spider, we humans struggle to make sense of the
vast and ultimately incomprehensible world around us. What we
call adventure is any journey we take into unknown territory.
Whether we shall ever arrive at a final, definitive truth about our
world is unlikely. What is certain is that we can embrace both the
gifts and vexations of being human and get on with the journey,
committed to enjoying every step of the way.

Make Your Own Adventures

1. Escape to Celebrate

Cultivating an "attitude of gratitude" in a pressured, goal-
oriented work environment requires a willingness to experiment
with new forms of group communication. You've got to carve out
the time and allocate some resources in order to reinvigorate the
status quo. And you have to allow yourself and others to feel a lit-

tle awkwardness as you deliberately create a ritual of thankful-
ness in your corporate culture. Above all, don't confuse solemnity with seriousness. Believe it or not, the most effective
team-building events are also the most fun.

> *Escape to celebrate by taking your colleagues on a journey to the*
> *mountains, the sea, or a local bistro. The location doesn't mat-*
> *ter as much as a sense of adventure and the intent to put men-*
> *tal and emotional distance between yourselves and the daily*
> *work environment. Once settled in at your chosen retreat, form*
> *a circle and place a "talking stick" in the center. Whoever holds*
> *the stick has the floor, and everyone should get equal time. Give*
> *everyone the opportunity to talk about what you most appreci-*
> *ate about the others in the circle, about the organization, about*
> *the job itself. The aim is to put complaints and worries aside*
> *temporarily while speaking from the heart about everything in*
> *your work experience that makes you want to say "Thank you!"*
> *The only rules:*
>
> - *No speeches.*
> - *Speak from the heart.*
> - *Keep it moving.*

Trust me, this technique works. I've seen the magic of gratitude manifest itself hundreds of times with some of the most
high-pressured, hard-boiled professionals on the planet. My
most recent experience was a daylong off-site adventure with a
senior management team from Wal-Mart. The retreat got off to
a good start when the two dozen usually staid and stressed executives running the largest retail operation on the planet conducted a forty-five-minute screaming water fight—complete
with Super Soakers and flying water bottles—on a moving
school bus. Later in the day, after a strenuous canoe paddle down
a remote river, participants formed a circle. As the talking stick

passed from hand to hand, the frivolous mood of the group began to shift. It was soon obvious that they all had long been waiting to express themselves in ways that a culture of intercoms and cubicles, tight deadlines and standard operating procedures prohibited.

As a circle of top-level managers of one of the world's most aggressive and successful corporations sat in a circle on a sweltering 100-degree Arkansas afternoon and revealed how much they cared about one another, a thought raced through my mind: buy Wal-Mart stock. Because I knew that these already top-producing professionals would be producing even more in concert as they returned to work with a markedly stronger attitude of gratitude.

2. BE STILL

We live increasingly preoccupied lives with little space left for wonder and reflection. Feeling up to here with nine-to-five jobs, commuting, child raising, and home maintenance, our lives may be so jam-packed by the mundane that we fail to perceive the sublime—which resides in all the subtle, mystical spaces where our busyness is not. Taoist sages were fond of saying that a pitcher wasn't made useful by the clay that formed it but by the space that the clay enclosed. That's the operating principle behind all forms of meditation: the mind needs to be emptied on a regular basis in order to receive new and useful insights and information.

> *Spend three minutes sitting in a comfortable position and deliberately empty your mind of all work-related and practical thoughts. You'll likely find that this process is much easier described than done, but don't judge yourself for your mind's tendency to keep itself busy. Instead of being captivated by your thoughts, simply watch them go by, like leaves floating down a*

river. You may find it helpful to tell your most insistent thoughts, "Not now, later." Try several three-minute sessions until you begin to notice the pace of your thinking slowing down. Then, go for five minutes; as your comfort with stillness increases, gradually increase the time you allow for meditation. If, like me, inactivity is not your strong suit, then try a form of active meditation: running, walking, rowing, dancing, or yoga. Start with half an hour of focusing on the motions of the activity instead of your thoughts. Every now and then, rise an hour early to watch the sunrise with as much "emptiness" as you can muster. Make it a regular practice to stop the world.

For years I left home with just enough time—if I drove like a demon—to make a flight to a scheduled speaking engagement. After the job, I arrived at the airport with precious few minutes before my flight back, and then tried to squeeze in a dental appointment or haircut before rushing home. What I told myself was that I didn't have a second to spare, but curiously, the more time I saved by rushing about, the less I seemed to have.

One day, exhausted and breathless as usual, I realized that while I was busy saving time, I was losing the joy that made life worth living. I was so busy going places I was never really arriving anywhere with full awareness of myself and the immediate environment.

These days I arrange my schedule so that I always show up a few minutes early for a flight, appointment, or even a movie. The extra minutes are scheduled in not to achieve anything but as opportunities to reclaim time by allowing my mind to come to a full stop and become more open to chance encounters, to unexpected sights and sounds, or to nothing at all. These moments are my opportunities for mini-meditation, and they help me slow down the pace of life while not slowing my effectiveness at all.

Remember: it's when you feel that you can least afford to take a breather that you're about to run out of air. Whether you call it meditation, your "mental health time" or a sacred space, try writing in regular appointments with "Nothing" in your day planner. Practice the fine art of hurrying less and living more.

3. ENJOY THE PROCESS

Life becomes an adventure whenever you shift your orientation from goals to process. It's not where you're going but how you get there that really makes life interesting. To test this proposition, try the following:

> *Head out . . . it doesn't matter where. Just walk out the door without a destination in mind and resist your habitual routes to work, the coffee shop, or the corner store. Be alert to whatever is going on around you and turn left or right or continue straight ahead, following only your momentary intuitions, hunches, and gut feelings. Try this wandering for an hour or two, then for an afternoon, then for an entire day. Strengthen your skill at being destination-free and see where it takes you. Most important, allow pleasure to be your guide. Enjoy the feeling of simply being.*

You can apply this exercise on your next business trip to some exotic location by just stepping onto the street and saying "The adventure begins!" Hop a bus or grab a subway to the end of the line. Wander into museums, bookstores, art galleries, neighborhood sandwich shops, the Greyhound station, a mission for the homeless. Take all the time you need and be open to chance conversations and invitations. If you happen to be driving, leave your maps behind and travel on instinct. Don't miss the opportunity to read historical landmark signs, stop at small markets, even join in a hot bingo game at a church or community center. You'll learn things about yourself that you never knew—and one of those things will surely be your natural proximity to joy.

A man who lived his life by enjoying the process was the late Linus Pauling, the only individual to win two unshared Nobel Prizes. Activist, humanitarian, and scientific maverick, he has been called by one biographer the "quintessentially American Great Man, brilliant, undisciplined, rebellious . . . unshakably confident in his own genius." I had the privilege of visiting with Dr. Pauling at his Big Sur home during the summer of 1994 while developing a video project. It was to be his last interview. Within a month, Dr. Pauling passed away.

He was alone in the house when I arrived. I first saw him, wizened and pale, lying in his bed surrounded by stacks of books on every side. A huge, two-handled magnifying glass was suspended from the ceiling. At ninety-three years of age he was still busy reading, studying, and exploring. Raising himself with shaking arms, he greeted me warmly and motioned me toward the living room.

When I raised the subject of adventure, Dr. Pauling chuckled. "Oh yes, there is much to discuss." His moist gray eyes sparkled beneath his famous black beret; the plumes of silver hair, unkempt and curling below his collar, and angular features combined to give him the look of a great grandfather eagle.

"I got the Nobel Prize for Chemistry in 1954 for my work on the nature of the chemical bond," he recalled. "I'd just been enjoying myself doing X-ray crystallography and applying quantum mechanics to chemical problems. Basically, I was just having a good time and I get the Nobel Prize for it!"

He also told me, with pride, about how his passport had been lifted during the McCarthy era because of his antiwar activism and opposition to the testing of nuclear weapons. As we spoke it became clear that Pauling was above all a compassionate man who had enjoyed his journey through life and advised others to do the same.

"I tell young people who may ask about a career: Look around and think of what you've done and decide what you like best. Then see if you can't make a living doing it."

At the end of the hour, with Pauling obviously tiring, I posed a final question. What had been the major motivation in his life? Ambition? Service? The need to leave a legacy?

"Curiosity has been the driving force in my life," he responded without a moment's hesitation. "And the pleasure that I get from understanding something that I had not understood before—or that nobody has understood before."

Pauling smiled. "It just gives me a lot of pleasure to make discoveries."

Epilogue

The mountain was known only as the satellite of Mount Bertrand. It had no real name, and no one had yet climbed it. Six years had passed since McAndrews and I had been halfway up the east face when an ice wall halted our progress. The mountain grew larger as I made my way across the Upsala Glacier; I was back and this time I was alone. Halfway through the day I passed a flat area among the crevasses. It seemed to be the spot where my strength had given out on the first trip, forcing both of us to spend a night on the open ice without a tent.

Gracious as always, McAndrews had never complained. That night we had lain on our backs on the ice staring up into the heavens, thanking the lucky stars above for good weather.

Now I hurried among blue and white towers, threading the final stretch of the maze. As evening shadows spread, blankets of cold rose from the ice. An hour before dusk, I reached dry land and stood in the loose boulders at the foot of the moraine.

I scrambled up the few hundred feet of loose talus in the day's last light and stepped into a lost world. Suddenly, the air was sweet with the breath of living things. The sterility of glacier and

scree was far below. I emerged into a lush island of virgin meadows and forest surrounded by a frozen sea of ice. It was unlikely
that anyone had set foot here since my visit with McAndrews
years ago. Tonight I had this paradise to myself.

I pitched my tarp by the side of a peaceful stream. The massive snow mountain above glowed faintly. I would take a different route from the one McAndrews and I had chosen; the north
side of the peak was a steep ridge of snow and rock that looked
unstable, but there was no other option. By the light of my head-
lamp I scrawled a hasty note to carry to the summit. I fell asleep
easily and awoke at 3 A.M. to prepare for the climb; by four I was
climbing in knee-deep snow.

The ridge route up the big mountain was steep, punctuated
with a few short snow walls and pinnacles of shattered rock.
Knife-edge narrow, with a drop of thousands of feet on each side,
my chosen path yielded no room for detours.

My concern was that any one impasse would be enough to
end the climb. By midafternoon I had climbed a full ten hours
and the mountain seemed only to be growing taller. In a sunny
niche, sheltered from the gusts of wind-borne powder, I used my
axe to liberate a trickle of snowmelt from behind a sheet of ice. I
refilled my water bottle and pulled a chunk of mutton from my
pack. Three minutes later, lunch was over. Time to move on.

The dreaded impasse never appeared. The final ridge was a
clean white curve to the summit bisected by a negotiable ice wall.
I chopped a few narrow steps to help secure a place for my
crampons.

At five o'clock, I stepped to the summit.

I knew what I was supposed to do. Steadying my pack in the
wind, I posed for documentary photos. I looked all around me:
the world was untrammeled and white. Forty-five miles to the
northwest, FitzRoy, already catching the first slanting rays of the
setting sun, glowed an unearthly purplish red. The little patch of

snow and rock on which I stood seemed ridiculously insignificant; my tired mind was only dimly aware of what I was doing here. The wind was growing fierce. It had taken thirteen hours from my camp to get here, and now all I could think about was the long, dark, dangerous evening ahead. I started down, then remembered the scrap of paper in my pocket: the reason I had come. I began to read, shouting the words into the wind that tried to tear them from my hands.

"How are you, my friend? Wherever you are, I just want you to know that you are with me, with all of us always. This hill is for you."

I shouted how much I loved him. I shouted to all creation my love of the whole crazy process of living and dying. I shouted my thanks for beautiful moments like this one, and for everyone I had ever loved and all I had ever learned. I asked only that I be guided off the mountain so that I might love and learn some more. Then I wrapped the note around the shaft of my ice ax and plunged it into the snow. Tears iced my cheeks.

I made it down safely. A sixth sense seemed to guide me handily around crevasses concealed beneath the snow that could have easily swallowed me alive. Someone seemed to whisper over my shoulder, warning me of every hidden patch of ice that would have sent me skidding off the ridge into a fatal darkness. Descending to the flanks, my weight repeatedly broke through the crusts of frozen snow until my gaiters ripped and my exposed shins, bruised and torn, left a trail of blood along the snow. I never found my tent. An hour of mucking around in the marsh by flashlight long after midnight failed to disclose the location of my camp. I stuck my mittens over my feet, my feet into my rucksack, wrapped myself around a bush, and fell into a delicious sleep.

The night was brilliantly starlit and bitterly cold. Uncomfortable but not unhappy, I awoke several times, let out a laugh, and went back to sleep. Despite my chattering teeth, I was filled with joy. Exposed to the elements without the security of warm bag or shelter, stranded on an atoll of forest between a huge rock and an ocean of ice—a long way from anything that resembled home—I felt not a tinge of fear or loneliness. Instead there was the unmistakable sensation of companionship.

I dreamed I was singing a song and woke myself up singing. My feet looked ridiculous as I pulled them from my rucksack, like woolly clubs with opposable thumbs. I found my sleeping bag and tarp over a rise, not fifty feet away.

Above me, Mount Steven McAndrews shone like gold in the first light.

RECOMMENDED READING

Aguayo, Rafael. *Dr. Deming: The American Who Taught the Japanese about Quality.* New York: Simon and Schuster, 1990.

Allison, Stacy, and Peter Carl. *Beyond the Limits: A Woman's Triumph on Everest.* Wilsonville, Ore.: BookPartners Inc., 1999.

Anderson, J. R. L. *The Ulysses Factor: The Exploring Instinct in Man.* New York: Harcourt Brace Jovanovich, 1970.

Ballard, Robert, and Rick Archbold. *The Discovery of the Titanic.* New York: Warner Books, 1998.

Brenner, Paul. *Health Is a Question of Balance.* Idyllwild, Calif.: Continuum Press, 1998.

———. *Seeing Your Life through New Eyes.* Hillsboro, Ore.: Beyond Words Publishing, 2000.

Buckingham, Marcus, and Curt Coffman. *First Break All the Rules.* New York: Simon and Schuster, 1999.

Buelcher, Han C., and Judith Maria. *The Bolivian Aymara*. New York: Winston, 1971.

Bynner, Witter. *The Way of Life According to Lao Tzu: An American Version*. New York: Perigee Books, 1995.

Campbell, Joseph. *The Hero with a Thousand Faces*. Princeton, N.J.: Princeton University Press, 1990.

———. *Myths to Live By*. New York: Viking Press, 1972.

Catford, Lorna, and Michael Ray. *The Path of the Everyday Hero: Drawing on the Power of Myth to Meet Life's Most Important Challenges*. Los Angeles: Tarcher, 1991.

Chatwin, Bruce. *In Patagonia*. New York: Penguin Books, 1979.

Collins, James, and Jerry Porras. *Built to Last: Successful Habits of Visionary Companies*. New York: HarperCollins, 1994.

Covey, Stephen. *Principle-Centered Leadership*. New York: Simon and Schuster, 1991.

Csikszentmihalyi, Mihaly. *Flow: The Psychology of Optimal Experience*. New York: HarperCollins, 1990.

Dass, Ram, and Stephen Levine. *Grist for the Mill*. Berkeley, Calif.: Celestial Arts, 1998.

Daumal, Rene. *Mount Analogue*. Baltimore: Penguin Books, 1974.

Dychtwald, Ken. *Age Wave*. Los Angeles: Tarcher, 1988.

Eiseley, Loren. *The Immense Journey*. New York: Vintage Books, 1957.

Eliade, Mircea. *Shamanism: Archaic Techniques of Ecstasy*. Princeton, N.J.: Princeton University Press, 1972.

Frankl, Viktor. *Man's Search for Meaning: An Introduction to Logotherapy*. New York: Simon and Schuster, 1959.

Greenleaf, Robert. *Servant Leadership: A Journey into the Nature of Legitimate Power and Greatness*. Mahwah, N.J.: Paulist Press, 1977.

Guiraldes, Ricardo. *Don Segundo Sombra*. New York and Toronto: New American Library, 1966.

Gushiken, José J. *Tuno, El Curandero*. Lima, Peru: Ediciones de la Biblioteca Universitaria, 1979.

Harner, Michael. *The Way of the Shaman*. New York: Bantam, 1982

Hawley, Jack. *Reawakening the Spirit in Work: The Power of Dharmic Management*. San Francisco: Berrett-Koehler, 1993.

Hayward, Jeremy. *Sacred World: A Guide to Shambhala Warriorship in Daily Life*. New York: Bantam, 1995.

Hendricks, Gay, and Kate Ludeman. *The Corporate Mystic: A Guide for Visionaries with Their Feet on the Ground*. New York: Bantam, 1997.

Hernandez, José. *The Gaucho, Martin Fierro*. Buenos Aires: Editorial Pampa, 1963.

Jaworski, Joseph. *Synchronicity: The Inner Path of Leadership*. San Francisco: Berrett-Koehler, 1998.

Keen, Sam. *Hymns to an Unknown God: Awakening the Spirit in Everyday Life*. New York: Bantam, 1994.

Keen, Sam, and Anne Valley-Fox. *Your Mythic Journey: Finding Meaning in Your Life Through Writing and Storytelling*. Los Angeles: Tarcher, 1973.

Klein, Eric, and John B. Izzo. *Awakening Corporate Soul*. Lion's Bay, B.C., Canada: Fairwinds Press, 1999.

Kohn, Alfie. *Punished by Rewards*. New York: Houghton Mifflin, 1993.

Kozlovsky, Daniel G. *An Ecological and Evolutionary Ethic*. Englewood Cliffs, N.J.: Prentice Hall, 1974.

Krakauer, Jon. *Into Thin Air*. New York: Doubleday, 1997.

———. *Into the Wild*. New York: Doubleday, 1997.

Kriegel, Robert. *If It Ain't Broke, Break It: And Other Unconventional Wisdom for a Changing Business World*. New York: Warner, 1992.

Lame Deer, John, and John Erdoes, *Lame Deer, Seeker of Visions*. New York: Washington Square Press, 1994.

Leider, Richard J. *The Power of Purpose*. San Francisco: Berrett-Koehler, 1997.

Metcalf, C. W., and Roma Felible. *Lighten Up.* Reading, Mass.: Perseus Books, 1998.

Meyer, Pamela. *Quantum Creativity.* Chicago: Yezand Press, 1997.

Miller, Patrick. *A Little Book of Forgiveness.* Berkeley, Calif.: Fearless Books, 1999.

Neihardt, John G. *Black Elk Speaks: Being the Life Story of a Holy Man of the Ogalala Sioux.* New York: Washington Square Press, 1994.

Peters, Tom, and Robert Waterman. *In Search of Excellence.* New York: Harper and Row, 1982.

Rebillot, Paul. *The Call to Adventure.* San Francisco: HarperSan-Francisco, 1993.

Saint-Exupéry, Antoine de. *Wind, Sand and Stars.* New York: Harcourt, Brace & World, 1992.

Shipton, Eric. *Eric Shipton—The Six Mountain-Travel Books.* Seattle: The Mountaineers, 1990.

Slater, Philip. *The Pursuit of Loneliness: American Culture at the Breaking Point.* Boston: Beacon Press, 1990.

Smith, Tony. *Parzifal's Briefcase: Six Practices and a New Philosophy for Healthy Organizational Change.* San Francisco: Chronicle Books, 1993.

Snyder, Gary. *Turtle Island.* New York: New Directions, 1974.

Stoltz, Paul. *Adversity Quotient: Turning Obstacles into Opportunities.* New York: John Wiley and Sons, 1997.

Thoreau, Henry David. *Walden.* Princeton, N.J.: Princeton University Press, 1989.

Trungpa, Chogyam. *Shambala: The Sacred Path of the Warrior.* Boston and London: Shambala, 1988.

Waterman, Robert. *What America Does Right: Learning from Companies That Put People First.* New York: W. W. Norton, 1994.

Watts, Alan. *Cloud-Hidden, Whereabouts Unknown.* New York: Random House, 1974.

———. *Zen: The Best of Alan Watts* (video). New York: Wellspring Media, 1994.

Whyte, David. *The Heart Aroused.* New York: Doubleday, 1994.

Wing, R. L. *The Illustrated I Ching.* New York: Doubleday, 1982.

INDEX

Way *of* Adventure

programs and products provide a wide range of resources for individuals, families, business, government, and educational organizations.

For information on bringing

Way of Adventure Trainings and Seminars

to your organization . . .

or to learn more about *Way of Adventure:*

- Training videos
- Himalayan Expeditions for Executives
- Keynotes with Jeff Salz

Please contact us online at:

w a y o f a d v e n t u r e . c o m